Blind to Misfortune

BLIND TO MISFORTUNE

A Story of Great Courage in the Face of Adversity

Bill Griffiths
with
Hugh Popham

ISIS
LARGE PRINT
Oxford

First published in Great Britain 1989
Reprinted in 1993 by Leo Cooper
This edition published 2005 by Pen & Sword Military,
an imprint of Pen & Sword Books Ltd.

Published in Large Print 2006 by ISIS Publishing Ltd.,
7 Centremead, Osney Mead, Oxford OX2 0ES
by arrangement with
Pen & Sword Books Ltd.

British Library Cataloguing in Publication Data
Griffiths, Bill
    Blind to misfortune. – Large print ed.
    (Isis reminiscence series)
    1. People with disabilities – Great
    Britain – Biography
    2. Large type books
    I. Title II. Popham, Hugh
    362.4'092

ISBN 0–7531–9374–4 (hb)
ISBN 0–7531–9375–2 (pb)

Printed and bound in Great Britain by
T. J. International Ltd., Padstow, Cornwall

For
My Wife Alice,
Our Family
and
St Dunstan's

Contents

Foreword..ix

Introduction xiii

1. "For God's sake, put me out!" 1

2. The Joys of Homecoming 63

3. Back to Work....................................101

4. A Fresh Start 118

5. This is Your Life 140

   Postcript: Return to Java 223

   Appendix 229

Foreword
by

Sir Edward Dunlop, A.C., C.M.G., O.B.E., K.C.S.J., M.S., F.R.C.S., F.A.C.S., F.R.A.C.S., LLd.D. Hon. Melb., D.Sc. Punjab (Hon.) Hon. Fellow of the Colleges of Surgeons of Thailand and Sir Lanka.

In Java, 1942, as Commanding Officer of a hastily improvised Allied General Hospital, as the victorious Japanese closed in, I was required both to establish priorities for treatment and to lead an operating team in dealing with a rush of casualties. The bomb-shattered body of a young man, L.A.C. Griffiths, posed special problems. His eyes were shattered in the wreck of his face, his hands blown away, one leg with a severe compound fracture; he was peppered everywhere with imbedded fragments, and was exsanguinated and shocked. Surprised that he should have reached hospital at all, I took the rather illogical decision to allot him top priority, and to treat him myself. His torn blood-stained clothing removed, it seemed less than kindness to try to prolong his life.

As the faint thread of life responded following lengthy operations, there began the awful challenge of his total helplessness for even the most basic bodily functions, and the blank wall of darkness and the hopelessness of the future. I was confronted by his distressed, compassionate Dutch nurse who said, "Colonel, Bill wants to die. If you do not have the guts to kill him, I will"! Even this flickering candle of life seemed precious in a world collapsing about us in which many or all of us might die. I sternly forbade this solution.

Subsequently at the time of the savage, sudden break-up of the hospital, I was obliged to stand between Bill and the bayonets of Japanese guards who regarded him as expendable.

Somehow he survived on a mixture of Lancashire pluck and the easy camaraderie in those camps of semi-starvation and death. There was almost no communication with home, but he built up hopes of taking up the threads of family life and of entering the family transport business.

Home proved an even greater test of his courage. His marriage had collapsed, the business had gone, and his widowed mother was beyond bearing the strain of his personal care.

Ironically the long-promised artificial limbs seemed useless to an eyeless man.

Encouraged to go to St Dunstan's, he found life began to dawn again. He enlisted his brother in the physical side of his successful transport business in which he handled the finance, business planning, telephone and typing. Alas, the nationalization of transport came as a cruel, disastrous blow to this enterprise.

Undeterred, he took up singing with the help and instruction of Alice, whom he eventually married, and the two of them became a wonderful team, not only as entertainers, but as inseparables, solving all difficulties — a totally inspiring pair.

In time, he has succeeded the famed Douglas Bader in the British mind as "Mr Disabled Man of Courage". He has become, of all things, "Mr Disabled Sportsman of the Year", has been accorded the tribute of "This is your life", and has been decorated with an M.B.E. by the Queen. He has travelled widely overseas, accompanied by Alice, a splendid ambassador for, and representative of, St Dunstan's. He has made several visits to Australia, has returned to Java and has been to "Hellfire Pass" in Thailand.

This totally remarkable man, who has overcome a very limited education and appalling disabilities to become a national inspiration, humbles us all. I count him and Alice as very dear friends who command my deep affection and admiration.

Among other attributes of his warm and generous heart is a total absence of bitterness or envy, and a capacity for helping others and of forming close friendships at all social levels. Among them are ex-servicemen of several Allied Nations.

I commend this book confidently as a record of heroic courage and fortitude shown by a young man whose astonishing victory over blindness and handlessness is an inspiration to us all.

Inseparable in our admiration and affection are "Billy and Alice" who are truly national treasures and are part of the pride of Blackpool.

Introduction
by

Admiral of the Fleet Sir Henry Leach
Chairman of St Dunstan's

Among some 6,000 blinded ex-servicemen and women who have come to St Dunstan's over the past 73 years there are any number of remarkable stories of success in overcoming the handicap of blindness and in integrating into the community, working with and for sighted people on equal terms.

One of the outstanding stories is told in this book. Bill Griffiths has succeeded in the face of a terrible double disability: the loss of both hands as well as total blindness.

St Dunstan's can provide training and opportunities. What it cannot do is provide the will and the effort. These must come from the St Dunstaner himself.

Bill Griffiths showed his powers of determination in the terrible years he spent as a prisoner of the Japanese. He has continued to do so over the years since then. Honoured by Her Majesty the Queen with the award of the M.B.E. by television's 'This is Your Life'; and by selection as the Disabled Sportsman of the Year, Bill has remained unspoiled.

He has continued his work, shared with Alice, his wife, travelling the North of England speaking on the work of St. Dunstan's. Together they charm their audiences with songs as well as words. At St Dunstan's we receive many letters of appreciation from people whose attitude to life has been changed by their example:

"We all enjoyed his talk immensely and were very much impressed by his magnificent spirit in the face of his cruel disabilities. We were also very appreciative of Mrs Griffiths' courage and devotion in helping him to surmount his troubles so splendidly. I think most people who were there will think twice about letting their own so much smaller troubles get them down in future. It was a truly inspiring meeting."

St Dunstan's is proud to have two such ambassadors to represent this organisation and personify the spirit of blinded ex-service people.

CHAPTER
ONE

"For God's sake, put me out!"

Bill Griffiths settles down at his typewriter in his study in the house on the seafront at Blackpool where he and his wife Alice live. The study window looks out over the garden to the houses in the road behind, but he cannot see it, for he has no eyes. Everything he wishes to write must be in his head, and he cannot read over what he has just written. And as he has no hands, he has a metal rod like a skewer, the last inch bent over at a right-angle, strapped to the stump of each forearm. The typewriter is electric; there is a metal frame fitted over the keyboard so that each letter is in a separate little box. When he types, his two steel "fingers" skitter and rattle over the frame as he counts the lines, up or down, the letters, so many from the left hand or the right. He is surprisingly quick at it, and does not make many mistakes, though he has a tendency to run off the bottom of the page, for there is no device to tell him when he has reached it. He starts to type.

The Jap guards ordered us out of the lorries. By the side of the road was some camouflage netting, covering I didn't know what. There must have been twenty guards, all with rifles and bayonets, shouting and gesticulating; none of them spoke English, but it was obvious what they meant — clear away the netting or get a bayonet in your guts. Instinctively I knew it was deadly or they'd have done the job themselves, but what choice was there? I knelt down and gingerly grabbed the netting with both hands. I was scared stiff; I noticed the guards stood well back. I heaved at the netting, and there was a violent explosion. I was hurled backwards. I felt for my face and couldn't feel it. I thought, God, my face has been blown off; I must have said it out loud, because at the same moment — I remember this most vividly — I thought, if I can speak, how can my face have gone I felt excruciating pain in my arms, and in my right leg. I tried to get up and walk but my leg wouldn't support me and I went down. I was fully conscious. I heard a truck pull up, and English voices, and then I was being lifted into the back of it — but I couldn't see.

Lying there in the back of the truck, I heard someone ask about a hospital, and I remembered that on the outward journey before the explosion I'd noticed one, in the village of Garoet, and now I said, carry on to the bottom of the hill, turn right, and you'll see it on your left. But they must have thought I was delirious, because I heard the driver asking someone, but they couldn't understand English; so eventually they did as I said and found the hospital and carried me in.

Suddenly I felt terribly cold, as if I was being lowered into a vat of icy water — the result, I realized later, of loss of blood — and the pain in my arms was awful. I can remember pleading, "Please put me out. For God's sake put me out!" and a calm voice saying, "All right, my boy, we will", and at last I slipped into a merciful oblivion.

Some time later I regained consciousness, and the same quiet voice said, "We're going to move you to another hospital, quite near. You'll be all right." I didn't care, the words meant nothing; all I wanted was to be released from the pain and misery.

The place was western Java;
the date, 16 March, 1942.

ii

The imposingly-named No 1 Allied General Hospital, Bandoeng, to which Bill was taken, had been a hospital, in fact, for rather less than a month. Before that it had been a school, and its transformation had been largely due to the energy and resource of one man, Lieutenant-Colonel Edward Dunlop of the Royal Australian Medical Corps. Singapore had fallen a month

before, the Japanese were already closing in on
the islands of the East Indian archipelago and
the uncertainty and chaos of defeat were
heightened by rumour and counter-rumour.
Dunlop — now Sir Edward, but still universally
known by his nickname of Weary — had reached
Java only a month before Bill's disaster, after an
exhausting two years of medical staffwork all over
the Middle East, and having escaped successively
from Greece, Crete and Tobruk. Professionally,
he was first and foremost a surgeon, but he was
also a soldier, for he had had a commission in
the Auxiliary Medical Corps since 1934. Above
all, though, he was — and is — a man of
remarkable moral stature, with courage, human-
ity, and modesty as outstanding as they are rare.
Thousands of Allied servicemen, Bill Griffiths
among them, owe their lives to him, and regard
him with the most profound affection and
respect.

His task at Bandoeng was, as he says himself
in his *War Diaries*,[1] herculean:

"Now with the distraction of almost daily air
action, we bent ourselves feverishly to equipping
and staffing what became 1 Allied General
Hospital. Equipment was gathered from most

---

[1] The War Diaries of Weary Dunlop, E.E. Dunlop, CMG, OBE,
KSJ, MS, FRCS, FRACS, FACS, D.SC. (Punjabi) (Hon). Thomas
Nelson, Australia, 1986.

4

diverse sources, such as the debris lying about
the docks after timely diversion from Singapore,
scattered minor Medical Centres, salvage from
Sumatra, purchases from shops and very generous donations from our Dutch allies . . .
Casualties began arriving with staff and stores
and frequently in greater numbers than the
unpacked beds."

The nursing sisters belonging to the unit had
been evacuated, much against their will, and in
their place eighty Dutch "Helpsters" — VADs —
were recruited, under the command of Matron
Borgmann-Brouwer de Jonge, known to her
patients as Mickey. She and Dunlop, more than
anyone else, helped Bill to survive those first
ghastly weeks and hers was the first voice he
heard when he recovered consciousness. He
himself remembers only fragments of that time
and was hardly to know how fortunate in his
misfortune he was. Soon there would be no
hospitals, a diminishing supply of drugs,
anaesthetics and food, and only the incredible
resourcefulness and skill of a handful of doctors
and medical orderlies to hold the fragile line
between illness and injury, and death.

John Denman, a friend and fellow-prisoner,
has described Bill's first few hours at Bandoeng:

"Colonel Weary Dunlop, the senior medical
officer, came to see me, because a few weeks

5

earlier, prior to the Japanese landing, we had together reconstructed his operating theatre, but there still remained much to be done. However, at the outset of our reunion, Bill Griffiths was lifted from a blood-soaked truck into that improvised scullery and straight on to the operating table. Some two hours later Colonel Dunlop returned to me from his operating theatre, exhausted and very moved. He said that there was a 30–70 chance of saving Bill's leg; but he had removed the remains of both his eyes, tidied up the stumps of his arms — and tended Bill's agony and had listened to his prayers to be "put out" before the anaesthetic hushed his cries. It would have been so easy to have done that, and Weary Dunlop asked me and my friends, John Rae Smith and Hugh Moxey, if he had been fair to Bill to place him on the frightful path that would lie ahead. Weary listened to all our views, and I said that I believed that some miracle would restore Bill."

iii

Forty-five years after the event Bill attempts to recall those first few weeks, the start of a period of his life which, since, he has been only too glad to forget.

The first voice I heard in that hospital was that of Matron Mickey de Jonge. She spoke perfect English, and did her utmost to comfort me, but the reality was such a nightmare no one on earth could have comforted me then. I didn't know that my sight had gone for ever, and sensibly she didn't tell me, though, of course I did know that my hands had gone. My right leg was in plaster from foot to hip, and I've been told that the rest of my body was a mass of bandages. I must have looked like a mummy.

My leg and the other wounds didn't bother me, but my two arms were agony. There were five or six inches from my elbow to the stump, and the pain was so frightful I used to rest them on my stomach and roll from side to side. Such dreadful pain. I can remember thinking to myself, this can't be true, it must be a nightmare, if only I can wake up, and I rolled about and even flung myself right out of bed to try and wake from it. But it was no nightmare, and I didn't wake up; the pain just went on and on.

Mickey and some others in the ward dashed over to me and put me back into bed, and Mickey said, "Billy, what's the matter?" I told her I'd hoped to wake myself out of the nightmare of pain, but it was still there. The only relief was after the morphia injection which she gave me early each evening; then the pain vanished, and I lay back on my bed, relaxed and at peace. It was then I was able to think more calmly and clearly about my situation, and I said to her, "I can't accept being like this. I can't. Give me an injection, something, anything,

7

and let me drift peacefully away. It's no good. I can't spend the rest of my life a complete wreck."

She understood all too well, for she knew that when the Japs got organized she would be interned and God alone knew what would happen to us. She said, "I would do it, but I have to have Colonel Dunlop's permission. I can't do it without."

She must have told him, for that evening he came to see me. Things wouldn't be too bad later on, he said; I should get stronger, and I should come to accept my situation. What about my sight, I asked him; but, like Mickey, he was non-committal. I don't know whether she ever really asked him about finishing me off, but whenever I pleaded with her, she made excuses; she hadn't managed to have a word with him, and so on.

"You won't forget?"

"No, I won't forget," she said.

Each morning I came out of my doped sleep back to the awful reality of the pain in my arms, knowing that I should have to wait all day for my "shot". All day I lay rolling from side to side, and all I could say was, "What time is it? What time is it?" Nothing existed for me outside the pain and the longing for the evening and the moment when the morphia took effect and the pain stopped. That I was a prisoner of war of the Japs meant nothing to me. I knew they were there. I heard Japanese voices in the ward and guns or bayonets rattling. I knew there was great fear and uncertainty in the air, but I couldn't have cared less. And only afterwards did I learn how nearly my longing for death had come to be granted.

That was later, though, just before we were moved to Tjimahi. First, there was just this eternity of darkness and pain. A few days after I was wounded I began to realize the extent of my injuries and, in the very depths of despair, had no wish to go on living. Weary Dunlop managed to visit me quite often, despite the huge number of other patients — 1351, he says in his book — in the hospital, and his calm, confident words gave me my only flicker of hope. The Japanese, he said, would soon be defeated, and when I got home I would get the best medical treatment, and my excellent constitution would see me through. The pain in my arms would gradually ease and I would get stronger. On one of these visits he said, "Ernie Ford [now a St Dunstaner] tells me that you keep moving your leg; is it painful?" "Yes," I said, "but nothing like as bad as my arms." "Let's have a look." He tapped the plaster, found the place, and cut away a small portion to reveal an ugly great ulcer, which he was then able to treat.

One result of the explosion was that my face was speckled with powder-burns, and my body was peppered with countless small bits of shrapnel. An RAF Officer, Andrew Crighton, who had been seconded to the Intelligence Service, was given the job of removing them. He was an ideal choice, for he had a quiet, soothing voice, and a gentle touch to go with it. Every day he would come along with his tweezers and prod and pick at my well-punctured frame to nip out the fragments of metal — and, incidentally, give me a good scratching, for that was something else I couldn't do for myself. I got to know Andrew very well, and was able to pour out my woes and my fears for the future to him "Here am I," I said, "twenty-one years of age, with no sight, no hands, and for all I know only one leg. What use am I? How can I cope with this lot? I've asked Mickey to give me something to put me out of misery, but she won't. Will you ask Colonel Dunlop for me?"

But he refused to do it. Instead he tried to encourage me by saying that when I got home I would be fitted with artificial limbs, and, as for being blind, he knew blind people who got along all right. "It won't be half as bad as you think." It was through him that I learnt that my sight had gone for ever. I remember the feeling of utter hopelessness when he told me: not panic, not terror, just the certainty that I couldn't face life like that, and the sooner it was ended the better. And with it, the helplessness, for if no one would do it for me, how could I do it for myself? Even if, by some miracle, I could find the right drug I couldn't get it to my mouth.

As if all this wasn't enough, I wasn't able to pee, and had to have a catheter rammed down my penis every time I wanted to make water. Not very nice; though Colonel Dunlop said it was only the result of shock and would cure itself in time. And it did, in time.

Gradually I came to know others in the ward. There were about six other severely disabled chaps; one, an Aussie, had had most of his face blown off and had been terribly burnt, yet managed to be cheerful. "I've just looked at myself in the mirror," he said on one occasion, "and my face is a right mess. Reckon my

10

wife'll throw me out when she sees me. You're lucky in one way, Billy; at least you can't see yourself." He was the first person to make me laugh, and I can still remember my surprise at finding I could.

Another was Ossy Gannon, also in the RAF. He'd been blinded in the same place the day after me. He came from Wigan, not far from my home town of Blackburn, and we spent the whole three and a half years in POW camp together. Another lad had lost a leg; and the bloke next to me one eye. He used to say, "It would have been all right if we'd each lost one hand and one eye, then we could've made a pair." He died of malnutrition six months later. Everyone was kind and tried to comfort and reassure me; each evening Mickey would come and talk with great patience and understanding when she'd given me my morphia injection; but nothing that anyone could do or say at that time could lift the dead weight of depression, the utter sense of futility I felt. I did not want to go on living, and nothing could alter that. If only I could find some way.

iv

Bill had been in the hospital exactly a month when the Japanese cracked down. For the two preceding weeks they had steadily been making their presence felt, ordering the removal of all Red Cross identification marks, expelling the "Helpsters", forbidding all contact with people outside. Colonel Dunlop describes the climax of this campaign of repression and intimidation.

"On 17 April 1942 the increasing harshness of the Japanese flared to extreme brutality. Captain Nakazawa demanded the immediate breakup of the hospital with most of the patients to go to prison along with those medical staff not needed for the few remaining. All were required to move at once. In order to dissuade him, I conducted him with his guard to demonstrate the serious illness of many patients. First among these, Aircraftsman Bill Griffiths, blind, with a shattered face, amputated hands, and a broken leg. Together with him was another blinded lad and two patients paralysed from the waist down.

Captain Nakazawa motioned to the bayonets of his guard. There was a tense moment as I interposed my body before Griffiths and glared at Nakazawa.

The threat was then transferred to the paraplegics whose eyes were dark with fright in their sweating faces.

Sick patients with chest and abdominal wounds had their legs struck contemptuously: 'Man walk'."

John Denman adds to this characteristically laconic account of a characteristically courageous action by Dunlop: "The Japanese guard . . . raised his rifle with its stubby fixed bayonet, and putting "one up the spout" for luck, prepared to lunge. Weary Dunlop placed himself in the way, saying, "If you are going to do that, you must go through me first.""

"And so Bill Griffiths was transferred with John and Hugh and myself to the hospital at Tjimahi."

The Japanese had originally ordered that the hospital should be cleared in ten minutes. Dunlop succeeded in having it postponed until the next day. By superhuman efforts emergency treatment was carried out on those too ill to be moved; documents, records and instruments were smuggled out, and medical stores, which they had been forbidden to take, were distributed amongst patients and staff in small, inconspicuous packets. The sheer cold inhumanity of their Japanese captors was being imposed on the wretched patients of 1 Allied General Hospital. Dunlop sums up his feelings as the lame, the halt, the maimed and the blind were driven like cattle the 4½ miles to the next abode, a penal institution.

"Life had been too busy for us to feel the sadness of captivity, and something tinged with guilt and shame that our lives were in the hands of men who despised prisoners. I pledged myself to at least face them unflinchingly at all costs."

No one could have honoured that pledge more completely than he did.

The patients had, in fact, been divided up between a number of camps. To Bill the worst blow was that he was to be separated from the two people who had done most to bring him through the horrors of the first month, Mickey de Jonge[1] and Colonel Dunlop. They, and other friends, John Denman and Andrew, were there to see him, as he puts it, "bundled on to a stretcher and put into the back of a lorry" for the journey to Tjimahi. The first stage on the long road to survival was over, with nothing better in prospect.

Bill's narrative continues:

Off we went and soon arrived at this so-called hospital. I was unloaded and dumped in a corner on my own; no one took any notice of me, but I could hear people dashing about and the Japs yelling and screaming. I was bursting for a pee; but although I shouted, there was no one who knew how to help. I lay there, writhing in agony, feeling as if I was going to explode — and then the dam burst, as Colonel Dunlop had said it eventually would, and the relief! I, the stretcher, everything was soaked, but that was nothing compared with easing of my swollen bladder, and I never had to

---

[1] In his book, Sir Edward Dunlop has a footnote about Mickey de Jonge. She became active in the Dutch Resistance on the island, was captured and tortured, and he says, "only just survived."

have the catheter again after that. That was one small mercy to be thankful for.

Eventually I was moved into a ward. The beds were about a foot apart, and I was told there were forty or fifty of us jammed in there. My arms were still hurting like hell, and I suddenly realized with horror that tonight there would be no Mickey to give me my "fix", and no "fix". It was a shattering blow, and I got no sleep at all that night. Life had become even more unbearable — but what choice had I but to bear it as best I could? For me, then, it was one long night of pain, of unending darkness like the grave. Only, unfortunately, I was still alive.

They called Tjimahi a hospital, but it was a prison. The VADS who had looked after us at Bandoeng had been interned, and although, fortunately for us, there were several doctors, Dutch, Australian and British, all the nursing had to be carried out by our own fellow-prisoners, some of whom had been nurses or medical orderlies before. I was allocated someone to look after me by the British Senior Medical Officer, Lieutenant-Colonel Peter Maisey, and he made a good choice. His name was Joe Holland, a soldier my own age, a smashing chap; what's more, he came from Burnley, quite close to my home town, so we had plenty to talk about. The other blinded bloke, Ossy Gannon, was in the bed across the ward from me, and he had a chap from Clacton-on-Sea, Walter Brazier, to care for him.

Joe Holland had been a postman in civvy street, and we used to natter away while he was feeding me the rice which was really just about all we got to eat; rice by itself, rice with what tasted like seaweed, rice, rice, rice. God, were we hungry! In fact, it was when I began to realize that I was actually looking forward to meals, boring and disgusting as they were, that I realized also that I must have started to recover from the shock, physical and psychological, of my injuries. Talking of food, during the whole time I was a POW I think we only had one hard-boiled egg between three of us — about once every six months — and I only remember having a bit of meat once. Very tasty it was too. Later someone told me it was roast cat!

But to get back to Joe and our chats. As I said earlier, I came from Blackburn where my grandfather had built up his own haulage business. Starting by selling fish, he'd moved into greengrocery, then bought a coach, and finally had a fleet of ten lorries. The firm was called William Griffiths (Blackburn) Ltd., and when I joined it on leaving school at fourteen, it was being run by my father and his brother. I'll tell you a bit more about them by and by. Until I got my licence when I was seventeen, I was what we called "Second Man" or driver's mate. But once I'd passed my driving test, I got to driving a lorry myself, all over the North of England, up to Scotland, down to London. I loved the work; life then was full of fun and excitement; sport, especially swimming, cycling, Saturday night dances. There was a whole crowd of us used to go, and Alice, who's now my wife, tried to teach me to dance; she sang with the dance band, too. Then we used to go dancing in the Winter Gardens in Blackpool, which I remember from holidays as a child — so that now, as I write this, although I can't see the Promenade and the Tower and the sands stretching out at low tide, I can visualize it all in my mind as it was then, when I was young and life was just beginning and full of promise. Alice and I were friendly and it might have developed — she says now I was only interested in her as a dancing-teacher! — but anyway another girl came on the scene and Alice was too shy to do anything about it. So Ethel, the "other girl", and I got married. Our daughter, Eileen, was born towards the end of 1940, and in January, 1941, I was called up, after deferred service, and joined the RAF.

Joe was feeding me my rice and talking about *his* wife and how worried he was about her, and I realized that I hadn't given a thought to Ethel and my little girl since I'd been wounded. I'd been totally cut off from everything that had happened before, imprisoned, not only in a Jap POW camp, but also in blackness and pain. Now, bit by bit, as Joe and I swapped banter about our respective home towns, and I talked about my transport days, slowly over the weeks that past would start to come back to me — and with it the dawning knowledge that it was gone for ever, that I should never sit behind the wheel of a vehicle again, but was destined to be spoon-fed and have my bottom wiped like a baby for the rest of my life.

For everyone, being in a Japanese POW camp was like living on the lip of an active volcano; for Bill, it was the same, but blindfolded and with his hands tied behind his back. He could constantly hear the guards stamping and shouting and brandishing their rifles and bayonets; or they would stop by his bed and jabber away at him, but neither made any sense or pattern to him, merely created a continuous sense of fear, of unease, of apprehension. Sometimes one of them would creep up on him and tickle his toes or his neck; and once he lashed out at his tormentor, which set the whole ward on tenterhooks, though nothing happened. Or they would come crashing into the ward and order everybody to stand up, no matter what their illness or injuries. When they tried it on him and he didn't move, they jabbed a bayonet in his ribs, bawling at him, "Man stand up!" until one of them pulled back the cover and saw his leg and they contented themselves with yelling at him instead.

Another of their little tricks was to make everyone stand in line and hit the man next to him; and if the guards thought anyone wasn't doing the job properly, they'd beat both of them up. To lie there, as Bill had to, listening to scenes like this going on, never knowing if it might be his turn next, was to live in a world of nightmare. The one consolation was the sympathy shown to him by everyone, fellow-patients and doctors alike: all of them — well, nearly all of them — would drift over and chat, trying to take his mind off his injuries, or help him become reconciled to them.

All this time Bill had been confined to bed, but after six weeks or so in Tjimahi one of the Dutch doctors, Dr Belmonty, decided that the time had come to remove the plaster from Bill's leg. This was the test of Dunlop's prediction of a 30–70 chance of saving it, for both tibia and fibula had been shattered, and such a double fracture does not mend easily, even under ideal conditions.

The tension, as Dr Belmonty began the delicate process of cutting through the plaster cast, spread to the other patients, and they hovered around near Bill's bed, awaiting the verdict. At last it was off; and there was the leg, a little shrunken and wrinkled, but healed. "Excellent, excellent!" Dr Belmonty pronounced when he had finished examining it, and a cheer went up from the spectators. "In one week you must try to stand on it a little."

The knowledge that he would at least have two legs, that, for once, the worst had not happened and that, at last, he would be able to move about, marked the first faint alleviation from the despondency that had clouded his spirit ever since the explosion. Gradually, too, the pain in his arms was beginning to ease, the frightful, remorseless, throbbing agony that had made him long for death and nothing else, had become an

19

ache, evil still but not all-consuming. The future, when he thought about it, held little enough promise, but the present had ceased to be beyond bearing and something of his old buoyant spirit began to revive. This is what is commonly known as courage.

vi

That week dragged by; but at last I was deemed ready to try putting my leg to the test. With Joe's help, I swivelled myself round, got one leg over the side of the bed, then the damaged one. Very gingerly, with Joe's help, I heaved myself on to my feet. I stood there tottering for a moment, and collapsed back on to the bed, all in. I'd been lying immobile for about two months, and that, with the lack of proper food, had made me as feeble as a new-born kitten, and I crawled back into bed and stayed there. But, having tried once, I had to keep going, so next day I made my second sortie, and this time I managed to creep round the bed and in at the other side — and that just about finished me. I suppose if I'd been able to see, or could have put out my hands to feel where I was going, it would have been easier; as it was, the stumps of my arms were still tender and painful, and, of course, I had no mental picture of where I was. It was like being in a pitch-black cellar full of obstacles through and round which I could only shuffle, one foot at a time.

Never mind. The old leg was holding up well, and there was usually someone about to guide me, or at least yell a warning if I was about to crash into something. Once I'd begun to get a sense of balance again, and my leg got stronger, I found the confidence to cast off from my bed and try walking up the ward. I didn't get very far the first time and suffered a few bumps in the process, but at least I was able to have a chat with some of the other patients who had only been voices in the distance to me up to that point. It was now that I heard at first hand of the ruthlessness of the Japs towards patients: an appendicitis case packed off to work within hours of being operated on, men almost too weak to stand, ditto, despite the pleas of the doctors. I also heard that Colonel Dunlop was in one of the camps at Bandoeng, where he had been joined by Laurens van der Post who had been with a guerrilla group up in the mountains and had been ambushed, only avoiding instant execution because he could speak Japanese and was able to address them with formal politeness! They were so amazed they spared him. In a funny way, knowing that Colonel Dunlop and Colonel van der Post were not far away, and receiving regular messages of encouragement from him through patients who had been transferred from his camp, was a tremendous source of strength to me; I owed it to Colonel Dunlop to go on living, and not to make the best of things would be letting him down. He's that sort of man, and I owe more to him than just my life.

With a few exceptions — and there'll always be a few miserable sods in any group like ours — the other fellows were great, especially a bunch of Welshmen of the 77th H.A.A. from the Rhondda Valley. They were grand lads, always ready to cheer me up or lend a hand when it was most needed. I'll not forget them. And there were many others who helped to sustain me and keep my spirits up through the three and a half long years of prison camp.

As my leg became stronger I became more adventurous, blundering about the ward and frequently bashing my nose or my shins as I went. In fact I hurt myself so much and so often, I tried walking backwards instead; at least that way I had a cushion when I ran into something! At this stage, though, I never left the ward alone. Either someone who could see would take my arm and we would go for a stroll; or sometimes Ossy Gannon, who was blind but had his hands and could therefore carry a stick, and I would set off arm in arm. He had learned his way about the camp after a fashion, and so we went tap-tapping our way round together. The place was crawling with Jap guards who had a habit of stopping us and shouting or giving us a clout. It was probably because we didn't bow to them, as they insisted every prisoner should. I certainly never did, not out of bravado; I couldn't be bothered; and oddly enough, I was rarely scared by them. Ignorance is bliss, perhaps; or it may have been that, deep down, I didn't really care whether I lived or died — as long as it was a quick death. On one occasion an Aussie by the name of Scotty Thomson took both Ossy and me out for a walk, one on each arm, and we ran into one of the guards. He did the usual yelling and screaming bit, and then thumped first Ossy and then me — but not the Aussie. This puzzled the three of us, and we finally worked out that it was because *we* had prevented Scotty from bowing because we were hanging on to him. A queer lot, the Japs.

vii

About this time, when I was beginning to feel a bit more cheerful — or at least not quite so despairing — and even, occasionally, to wonder what life might be like when the war ended, and whether I might not be able to find some place in it, I became afflicted with a strange feeling of unreality, accompanied by a severe and permanent headache. It felt as if my head was swelling up at the temples, and I developed the habit of stroking my forehead with my stumps, trying to feel if this was really happening. I couldn't concentrate, I kept on forgetting things, I felt light-headed, and my little bit of confidence leaked away, leaving me scared and apathetic. Perhaps I was going mad.

I didn't tell anyone, but found myself listening to my fellow-patients, to see if any of them had similar symptoms, and if anyone else complained of a headache I felt better about mine. It may have been delayed shock, or the lack of vitamins in our diet which affected different people in different ways; whatever the cause, it was very unpleasant, and I finally poured out my woes to one of the Dutch doctors who was reputed to be a psychiatrist. He listened sympathetically and assured me that for as long as I merely *thought* I was going bonkers I was all right; and, as if to prove the point, he took me over to a compound where there were a number of Javanese boys who really were as mad as larks — though they didn't know it. He suggested no treatment, and eventually the hallucinations and the headache stopped of their own accord, but it was a terrifying experience.

Now that I was no longer confined to bed I had to have my head shaved like everyone else. This was done in a hut some way from the ward and, on a later occasion when I was on my way there, I had an experience with one of the guards which illustrates just how baffling their behaviour could be. But by then I had my stick, and as this was one of the great moments, almost like finding I could walk, I must tell you about it.

Some of the prisoners devoted themselves to working out ways of helping those of us who were disabled and giving us some independence. They used materials, wood, wire, tin cans, smuggled into the camp, and decided to try and make me a holder so that I could carry a stick. They took two tin cans, removed the tops and bottoms, and riveted them together by means of a bracket which allowed some movement of my elbow. The top tin came above it, and the lower one protruded beyond my stump, and the stick slotted into it. I could slip it on by myself, and it was a tremendous boon. They made a similar gadget to hold a spoon, so that, for the first time, I was able to feed myself. I'm ashamed to say that, at first, I was reluctant to try them, but once I'd got the hang of it I used them all the time and was deeply grateful for them. When you're as reliant upon other people for the simplest actions of life as I am, anything that enables you to do things for yourself — this typewriter, for example — immediately allows you a measure of self-respect. Every tiny hard-won morsel of independence is precious.

Anyway, to go back to the "barber's shop". I was on my way there one day for the regular head-shaving ritual when one of the guards stopped me and asked in broken English "Where you go?" I told him, and he took hold of my stick, drew me to the side of the path, and said, "Sit!" I had learnt to be pretty wary of these jokers; you never knew when they were going to give you a clip over the ear or stick a bayonet into you; so I sat down and waited. After a bit he said, "No eyes. No hands. Leg not good. How come?"

"Booby trap, boom, boom," I said, and threw my head back and my arms up to illustrate what had happened. This seemed to irritate him, for he shouted at me, "Why you not die?" — as if surviving had somehow been my fault.

"Very good doctor saved me."

This seemed to annoy him too. "Is Doctor in camp?" I was beginning to get a little worried by this time. I couldn't make out what he was getting at. "No," I said, quite truthfully. He still wasn't satisfied. "What name doctor?"

Uh-uh, I thought. I'm not telling you, mate. "Don't know doctor's name."

He seemed to accept this; but then he gave a strange little sort of snort and said, "You want die." I wasn't sure if it was a statement or a question, but I said "No!" very emphatically, and shook my head to make it perfectly clear.

There was a short pause, and he said more quietly, "No eyes, no hands, you better dead." I shook my head again, and he put the muzzle of his rifle against my heart. "You better dead."

Oddly enough, I wasn't particularly frightened. I was fairly sure he wasn't going to shoot me there and then; but if not, was it some kind of warning, or his idea of a joke, like the ones who came and tickled my feet, or threw leaves and twigs and things into my face while I was walking about the camp?

I said nothing, just waited, and then, to my astonishment, he moved the gun away from my chest and said, "Now, hair cut!" I must admit it had gone clean out of my mind, and I'd have thought out of his.

That wasn't the end of it. As I went on my way to the barber's I could hear him following behind, giving a little cough from time to time as if to tell me he was there. When I reached the hut, he brushed past me; there was a lad already there, having his head shaved; the guard ordered him out to make room for me, and only then did he finally leave me in peace, and I wasn't sorry.

In all the time I was in POW camp there were only three other acts of kindness by guards that I remember. The first happened a few months after I was in Tjimahi. One of the guards came and sat on my bed and started jabbering away at me. This was so unusual, and he was so close to me, I thought for a minute he was going to strangle me or something. Not at all: he'd brought a bowl of *nasi goreng*, and, summoning Joe, told him in sign language to give it to me, which Joe did, while the guard sat and watched until the last grain of rice had been shoved into my ever-open mouth. Then away he went. I would have liked to have shared it with the others, as we did with any little treats that came our way, but the guard wouldn't have it; he'd brought it for *me*, and he was going to make darned sure I ate it! I may say I've enjoyed *nasi goreng* ever since.

Another time I was out on one of my wanders around the camp when a guard stopped me. I wondered what was coming this time, for he didn't utter a word. The next thing, I felt a cigarette being placed between my lips and heard him light it. Then he tapped me on the shoulder, as if to say, "Make the most of it" — which I may say I did — and went on his way. I thought I was on to a good thing, but although I made a point of walking that way from then on, it never happened again.

The third time was when we were due to leave Tjimahi and were kept standing in the blazing sun hour after hour and a Japanese officer brought me a chair to sit on. However, a few minutes later he came and took it away again — so I'm not sure that one counts!

Mostly, though, it was very different, as on the occasion when I was stopped on my slow plod back to the ward by a guard raving and bawling at me. I stopped, as I always did, and waited to see what was going to happen this time. I had a feeling that I'd been got at by this bastard before, though I couldn't be sure.

27

His voice became more and more hysterical, and I could hear him making purposeful noises with his rifle, and then I felt something cold and sharp being drawn across my stomach. Was he suggesting that I should commit hara-kiri? Usually I managed to keep my cool with them, but there was something about the way this so-and-so was going on at me that got my goat, and I faced him and said, "Piss off!" in a loud voice. Message received and understood! He gave me a hearty belt across both cheeks with the flat of his hand and went stamping off. The lads who were watching had been quite worried for a moment, but reckoned I'd won the round!

This kind of behaviour of theirs was nearly always in the back of my mind when I was out walking, but to be able to be out on my own was so important to me in coming to terms with my disability that I certainly wasn't going to let it deter me. There's no doubt that there was — perhaps still is, unless the leopard's changed his spots — a streak of callousness and cruelty in the Japanese character, as any ex-Jap POW will tell you, and from time to time they'd work it out on me.

One particular incident sticks in my mind. Again I was wandering round by myself, quietly whistling, when two guards closed in on me, one on either side, talking excitedly, and shepherded me along and into some room or other, I'd no idea where. Once inside, they closed the door; one of them snatched my stick and tin gauntlet off, and they both started gently prodding me with their scabbarded bayonets, and spinning me round in the process. Whether they were trying to make me dizzy or what I don't know: all I do know is that I'd gone beyond being scared and was sorely tempted to lash out at them — not that that would have done any good, in fact it would have made matters worse.

I could hear them giggling away to one another; but at last they seemed to tire of their baiting, opened the door, and pushed me out — without my stick. I started to shuffle off, feeling the edge of the path with my foot, when I felt something hit me in the back; they'd thrown my gauntlet and stick after me, and I didn't waste any time getting rigged up and escaping. I had completely lost all sense of direction, but after wandering around for a bit someone saw me and set me on the right path back to the ward. I didn't tell anyone about the incident for fear my walks might be curtailed — anything rather than that.

I know these were all small, unimportant examples of Japanese behaviour, a kind of cruel teasing really, and nothing compared to the sheer brutality they inflicted on the wretched prisoners they employed as slave labour, not only on the Burma railway or Ambon and Haroeke, building airstrips, for instance; but it was an odd way to treat someone as vulnerable as I was. I knew all about practical jokes, for I was a right monkey myself when I was a kid — knocking on doors and dashing off, altering the milk-tallies, tying two door latches together, that kind of prank — but we'd not pinch a blind man's white stick and throw it away or go out of our way to inflict pain on helpless people. Yet our Japanese guards, many of them, seemed to derive a sadistic pleasure out of humiliating and taunting us.

Once, early on in my walking days, it must have been, I must admit I rather asked for it. I always tried to memorize the route I took so that I could find my way back, but on this occasion I went badly wrong and the guards started yelling at me and finally manhandled me round and gave me a shove back the way I'd come. Apparently I'd been busy tapping my way out of the main gate!

Perhaps I'm making myself out to have been more cheerful than I really was. Inside, I was pretty miserable, especially when I tried to imagine what I was going to do when I got home; but as time went on and the pain in my arms became less and I was able to get about a bit, I was able to think about the others in the camp instead of just about myself and my disabilities, and I realized that, blind or sighted, whole or maimed, we were all in the same boat, basically, and they had a job to keep their spirits up, just as I did. It was then I resolved that, however full of despair I might feel, I would do my level best not to show it. That way I felt I might have a part to play in helping others, and so, as far as I could, I put on an air of cheerfulness, whistling and singing a bit as I wandered about, which I was often far from feeling.

"7 August, 1942. Bandoeng. About seventy arrived from Tjimahi Hospital, including some old friends . . . Bill Griffiths, the sightless and armless boy, now moves about cheerfully."

From The War Diaries of Weary Dunlop

"It was here I met one of the bravest patients of my whole war experience . . . To subsequently face the future of the Japanese onslaught and the life of a POW would require the greatest courage. Bill had that. He also had good and devoted friends to help him through the details of each day. A moment's reflection will reveal some of the horrors which were his. My part in his care was minimal whereas his lessons to us all were maximal."

Leslie Poidevin. Samurais and Circumcisions. 1985.

Apart from his various helpers — such as Andrew Crighton, from whom he was parted after the move to Tjimahi, Joe Holland, and the other blind Lancashire boy, Ossy Gannon — Bill remembers several of those "good and devoted friends" from one or other of the half-dozen camps and hospitals he was in in Java, and those who survived are friends to this day. One was John Denman, a major in the Prince of Wales Volunteers and an architect in civilian life. He

31

liked to talk about the houses he was hoping to
design when, at last, he was able to practise
again, and he and Bill would discuss plans and
garden lay-outs and all the things they hoped to
do when the war was over; but even while they
talked, Bill knew that it was all fantasy as far as
he was concerned. "We lived on dreams in prison
camp." Indeed, what else was there to live on?

One has to remember that Bill was only
twenty-one, and to be robbed of sight and hands,
a hideous deprivation at any age, seems doubly
cruel then. For this reason, perhaps, the friendship of older men was particularly important.
One was Alboin Smith, a male nurse in the RAF,
who, during the long nights when he was on
duty, would come and talk hour after hour as Bill
lay sleepless on his hard bed. A former
railwayman from Nantwich who had worked at
Crewe, he and Bill could yarn about places
which Bill had known in his lorry-driving days;
but more than that the older man possessed a
rare gift of sympathy, knowing as if by instinct
the emotional support the lad needed in his
lonely hell. "I looked upon him as a father-
figure," Bill says; and the awful isolation of the
blind and maimed in the hostile world of the
prison camps comes through. That brave assump-
tion of cheerfulness was as fragile as glass.

One tiny anecdote goes to the heart of it.
Alboin had managed to scrounge the leftovers
from the Japanese guards' supper and brought

them in triumph to Bill. "Billy," he said, "this is a sight for sore eyes!" — and then, realizing what he had said, went on worrying about it for years afterwards.

Then there was Harold Wilson, no politician, but a man who had kept a little village shop of the old kind that sold everything from soap to sausages and feather dusters to bananas, and which, at Long Bennington near Grantham on the old Great North Road, Bill had driven past at all hours of the day and night and remembered. He didn't talk a lot, but out of a natural simplicity and kindness, and with the experience of fifteen more years of life than Bill had had, he represented a decency and sanity which their world most notably lacked. "Without their example," Bill says, "I would never have survived," — and he is referring, not just to these two but to everyone who helped him, physically and emotionally, to survive those years.

ix

After about four months in Tjimahi, Bill, with two hundred other POWS, was moved to another camp. Since, like The Cat Who Walked By Himself, "all places were alike to him", it is difficult to work out his exact itinerary, but, Dr Poindevin says that he saw Bill in Tandjong Priok camp, on the outskirts of Batavia, some time between October, 1942 and January, 1943, and Bill remembers that particular camp, which was on reclaimed land near the docks and little better than a swamp in the wet season. During the three and a half years he was in at least six different places, including two former religious establishments — St Vincentius and Mater Dolorosa — "Cycle Camp", an old Dutch army camp in Batavia, and a place with the sinister name of Boe Glodok Gaol, also in Batavia.

What he does remember is being paraded before their departure and having to stand for over four hours in the burning sun — the occasion of the offered chair — then being taken by lorry to the railway station, and a five-hour journey to the next camp. He had had three weeks of freedom in Java between arriving, after a perilous three-day voyage from Singapore to Batavia, and being blinded; and now, as the train ambled through the lush green countryside which he could no longer see, he was able, as it were, to run his mental film of what he had seen then.

I constantly found myself recalling it, and in a strange way it seemed to give me a certain feeling of freedom which is difficult to explain. In my mind's eye I had a picture of the thronging streets of the city crowded with old and young, riding bicycles, pushing carts, chaffering at the market stalls, all the heat and colour and noise of the tropics which made an indelible impression on me. It was all so strange and new, another photograph in my mental snapshot album, which was already filling up with memories from the voyage out to Singapore in the *Cape Town Castle*: Cape Town itself, and Table Mountain; the streets of Bombay — where I lost a borrowed rupee on the oldest con of all, the three-card trick! — Colombo; then Singapore with the roadstead and Keppel Harbour jampacked with ships of every kind, and the city crowded with Malays and Chinese, music blaring out from the shops, smells of spicy food — and open drains — Chinese characters written up over the shops, rickshaws, the whole Mysterious Orient. What a tale I shall have to tell them back in Blackburn, I'd thought, after the war! That had all changed now. Instead of going home brimming with the tales of my adventures in the East, I should be an object of pity, at best, a burden at least. Best not to think about that. And there, beyond the boarded-up windows of the train, was the Java I remembered, the paddy fields and the jungle-clad mountains and valleys, the cheerful country people, and a crowd of children who waved madly as we drove past in the army lorries. The lads with me tried to peep through cracks in the boards and describe the country we were passing through, while I had my own private view of it. If it didn't happen to tally with the reality, so what?

As to the camps themselves, of course, I can only go by what the others told me. All of them, I believe, were brick-built with red-tiled roofs, but the camps were single-storey while the two Religious houses or schools, whichever they were, had two. I never felt safe in them; rightly so, because at St Vincentius, where I slept upstairs, I nearly came a fearful cropper. I'd been up and down the stone staircase — it had fifteen steps — hundreds of times, but on this particular day I was on my way down when my right foot slid off one of the treads, and I felt myself about to fall the rest of the way — so I jumped. That's to say, I pushed off with my other foot, with my arms across my face, and crashed to the bottom. More by luck than judgement I landed on my feet, but there was only a yard between the last step and the wall opposite, and I lurched into that. But I was in one piece, though very shaken (try jumping just a couple of stairs with your eyes tight shut if you want to know what it feels like; mine was a drop of about six feet) — and who should be there, watching the performance, but one of our charming Jap guards. And what did he do? Start bellowing at me, of course. It was a salutary lesson in not getting too cocky, and I treated those stairs with considerable caution after that.

One of the worst things about that first year was having nothing to do except mooch about, being sworn at in Japanese whenever I stepped out of line — or even when I didn't. It's enough to make anyone morbid. But then one of the Dutch doctors found a job for me. He had a dispensary in a small hut somewhere in the grounds; proper drugs and medicines were scarce, and he had got hold of various local medicinal herbs and roots which he wanted pounded together, and he thought I might be able to do it. After a certain amount of trial and error, I found I could just about grip the pestle with my stumps enough to crush the ingredients together, pick up the mortar like a woman with floury hands picking up a mixing-bowl with her wrists, and tip the contents into a sort of mixer which broke them down into a powder. I don't know if they did any good to anyone, but at least it gave me a useful occupation for an hour or two a day and that was the main thing from my point of view.

Then Colonel Maisey, the SMO, started employing me as a "runner", carrying messages around the camp to doctors, medical orderlies and so on. Some of them were written down; others were verbal and I had to commit them to memory. I also had to remember my way about in order to find the recipients, and I felt like a secret agent as I shuffled about the camp with these various messages concealed about my person. Not that I had anything much to conceal them under or in. When I first started walking, someone gave me an old pair of pyjamas, someone else gave me a bush-whacker hat, and a third person found me a pair of old wooden sandals, the sort that have a strip of cloth that slips over the top of your instep and keeps them on. Finally I came by a pair of shorts, and that was my "wardrobe" the whole time I was a POW. Oh, I also had the remains of a towel, which came in useful after my "bath", which consisted of me stripping off and the blokes throwing buckets of water over me.

I did try learning Braille using one foot to read with. I had this board, on which someone had fixed the raised dots, set up at the end of my bed, and I would use my toes to scan it. I got so far and then stuck. I couldn't see it being of much use when I was back in civvy street. But it gave me something to do. Seeing me doing it infuriated the guards, for some reason or other; they would stop and mutter at me, and on one occasion actually confiscated the board. They seemed to take exception to anything that was at all out of the ordinary, or which they didn't understand.

Although everybody, including me, at one time or another, went down with the usual tropical illnesses, malaria, dysentery, and dengue fever, etc, I did my best to keep fit. Every morning, if I wasn't actually ill, I would do my exercises, touching my toes with my stumps — and that means bending a lot further than simply touching them with your fingertips! — running on the spot, knees bend, stre-e-e-tch, and other ones I'd learnt doing PT in the RAF. The only one I couldn't do was press-ups.

In the various camps one met people from every walk of life, from tea and rubber planters to priests of every denomination, from teachers to solicitors to cooks and plumbers and drivers like me. I talked to them all and several of them gave lessons and lectures on their particular subjects which I attended, and if I'd managed to retain all I heard then I'd be a lot better educated than I am. But somehow the atmosphere wasn't conducive to study, not for me, at any rate. I feel now I missed a unique opportunity to make up for the years of schooling I didn't have by leaving school at fourteen. To think, I might have become quite an expert on the French Revolution if I'd paid more attention to one of the historians amongst us. His name was Leo Collier, and he came from Blackburn like me. A super bloke, I used to sit on his bed, and he would ramble on about Robespierre and Danton and Madame La Guillotine — it all sounded a bit like a Jap POW camp — but I found it enthralling at the time, even if most of it's gone now.

POW camp didn't have much to be said for it, but one thing it did do was throw together this tremendous mixture of people, people one wouldn't have met, probably, in normal everyday life, and who undoubtedly helped to broaden one's outlook. Funnily enough, though, as things turned out, I have met since, and still do meet, as wide a variety of people as I did then, but that's to run ahead of my story. And in most of them the shared misery of disease, hunger, discomfort, brutality and all the rest of it brought out the best.

But it wasn't easy for any of us to keep cheerful — or even sane. I developed a terror of being shut in anywhere, and this lasted for many years after I'd been released. One chap was everlastingly washing his hands, though there wasn't any soap; he was terrified of picking up various diseases; others suffered from what we called "dropped feet" and shuffled along without ever picking their feet up. And we were all obsessed by the subject of food. Not girls; we had no interest in them. Food! Whatever subject of conversation was started, it nearly always ended up on food; the lack of it, the delicious meals we'd had in the past and would have when we got back home; how we could manage to acquire more of it — some hope! I'd always had a voracious appetite, and I remember being always hungry as one of the worst things about being a POW: when release finally came I weighed less than 6 stone.

Remember, the majority of us were just young lads, and grub is one of the things young lads tend to be interested in!

But however grim our particular situation seemed, there were thousands of others far worse off. We knew nothing then of the horrors of the Sumatra mines, the building of the airstrips on the islands, of the Burma-Thailand railway, but I remember vividly the arrival of a bunch of prisoners from the islands of Ambon and Haroeke. Dr Poidevin writes of these poor devils:

> There is no doubt in my mind today that the sight of these bodies was the most gruesome that could ever be imagined. To see a man killed or shot or wounded or even see one die after treatment is always nauseating enough, but to see these parchment-like bodies, dead or dying of starvation and maltreatment is the most pitiable and shameful sight. "How dare the Japanese treat our men like this," was the thought of all who saw them. Even our Japanese hospital guards and the Sergeant were so horrified that their attitudes became helpful — for a while.

And Dr Poidevin quotes the report submitted by Dr John Lillie to Lieutenant Colonel Maisey on the five such drafts of working-parties, British and Dutch, which arrived at St Vincentius between 1943 and 1945.

> They had been on a journey which lasted one month in the hold of a tramp steamer and had just

completed the last lap with a 36-hour train journey. The men were extremely filthy and clothed only in rags, some were even completely naked . . . We carried about 200 men from the train who were unable to walk . . . the men in the carriages (60 in each coach) were absolutely helpless, doors and windows had been kept shut during the journey . . . nearly all were suffering from diarrhoea and dysentery . . . many had fallen from the seats to the floor and had to remain there.

Virtually every man was suffering from beri-beri and malaria and was swarming with body lice; many weighed as little as 70 pounds. And Dr Lillie's report continues:

These conditions were repeated with the arrival of each of the following drafts, reaching a climax with the final one in November 1944 which had been 68 days on its journey and had lost over 300 of their original 640 during the sea journey.

Those who died were, of course, simply thrown overboard. "These men," Dr Poidevin says, "had really been worked to death."

X

Altogether I spent three Christmases as a POW. They were pretty cheerless, though we did what we could to summon up the festive spirit. Not easy when, on one of them, we all got together to sing carols, and a couple of Jap guards came storming in, wielding their bamboo staves right, left and centre, and broke it up. They hated to see us enjoying ourselves, even in such a harmless way.

I can't remember whether it was that Christmas or another, but I do clearly remember lying on my bed one Christmas night and thinking that the same sky which looked down on us in our tropical imprisonment covered the old, familiar winter streets of home. I couldn't see those skies, but I could visualize them, the blue and the grey, the twinkling stars and the warm glow behind the black-out curtains. How far away it all seemed!

During the last two years at least a dozen of my fellow-prisoners looked after me at various stages. They were all sick men, that's why they were there; and long before they had recovered the Japs sent them back to work. The result was that I'd no sooner get used to a new helper — and he to me — than I found he'd been replaced by someone else. It can't have been any fun for them to be detailed to care for me, but they were wonderfully kind and patient and I hated it when one left and another took his place.

One of the problems with men weakened by starvation and especially those from Ambon and Haroeke was loss of willpower. We all felt it at one time or another; it was a real effort even to get off one's bed and walk about, but their dose was acute. I realized this, and, with the permission of the doctors, used to chivvy the chaps on to their feet and march them up and down the ward, "left-right", "left-right", like a sergeant-major. I suppose because I had forced myself to walk — backwards, very often! — they felt shamed into obeying. It was done as if it was a bit of a joke, really, as my old pals Les Stubbs and Jim Fraser would tell you; but the purpose was serious enough.

Towards the end of the war I was moved again, this time to Cycle Camp, a former Dutch army barracks near Batavia — now Jakarta. To me it was much like every other one I was in, but Dr Poidevin describes it in his book:

> The buildings were all of brick with red tiled roofs, grey tiled floors, very high ceilings and well-ventilated with doorways and large windows opening on to tiled verandahs on both sides of each large barrack. There were many rows of such large barracks with an ablution bench and an open drain lavatory for each hut.

Batavia was the port at which I'd arrived in the *Empire Star* in February 1942 — three years, and a lifetime, ago — but I could remember it all too well. In fact, I shall never forget that time.

After six pleasant, peaceful months in Singapore, suddenly the war arrived with a bang. Day after day Japanese bombers, in their standard pattern of three groups of nine, plastered the city and every military installation, including the aerodrome where I was stationed. Finally I was ordered to fill a lorry with men and take them down to the docks, and as I set off past the perimeter, I had had to veer off to the far side of the road to escape the heat and flames from the aviation fuel storage tanks which had been set on fire.

At the docks all was panic, havoc and utter chaos. There were fires everywhere, and millions of pounds worth of equipment of every kind was being pushed over the edge of the quays into the harbour. The troops scrambled out of the back of the lorry, and I was about to go back for more when a sergeant came across and said, "Leave your vehicle there, laddie, and get aboard that ship there and be quick about it!"

I saw him once more, saluting as we steamed out with bombs raining down all around us, and astern the ack-ack guns going all out, and the city under a dense rolling cloud of black smoke. On board we were packed like sardines, there was very little to eat, and when daylight came after a fairly peaceful night, and with it the bombers, we were all sent below into the hold. And there, in the dark, huddled together like sheep in a pen, we could hear the bombs come whistling down, feel the ship zig-zag, the sickening judder as she was hit. None of us, I think, expected to finish that voyage or come out of it alive; a number of ships were sunk or received direct hits. HMS *Birmingham* had one gun turret completely demolished, and our ship was hit twice and set on fire; several men were killed. For a time things looked serious; but the crew brought the fire under control and after 3 days of anything but first-class luxury, we reached Java, where, very soon, it was Singapore all over again.

There were a lot of brand-new army lorries on the quayside and my pal 'Johnny Powell' and I were detailed to deliver them to a compound for distribution to various aerodromes and camps throughout the island. After that we were given the job of loading a couple of trucks with ammunition and taking it to Bandoeng. We were in the process of loading when some Japanese fighters came over and started shooting up the ammunition dump. We nipped off smartly and took cover — though our "cover" turned out to be a wall made of attap — a sort of palmthatch — which was anything but bullet-proof! Then it was off again; this time, it was said, to some port from which we might escape once more, to Australia; but it turned out to be, like so many other rumours at that time, wishful thinking. For in our bones we all knew by now that for the Allies it was one more defeat, and we couldn't any longer fool ourselves that it wasn't. I can still remember the awful sinking feeling, the sheer sense of hopelessness, when we finally realized it.

Frank Jackson, another driver and I had driven our trucks up to Garoet in the mountains to pick up a party of RAF men who were stranded there when the news of the capitulation came through and up went the white flags. The RAF boys were in a school in the village and we joined them. There seemed to be nothing to do but sit tight and await developments. They weren't long in coming — a squad of Japanese soldiers, looking extremely arrogant and proud of themselves, who surrounded the school and prevented anyone leaving. Our captivity had begun; yet, at that moment, I think our main feeling was of relief that the anxiety and uncertainty were over. Suddenly matters were out of

45

our hands and few of us, I think, had any idea of what was in store for us, or even gave it much thought. But few people at that time could foresee the ruthless and brutal way in which the Japs intended to treat their prisoners.

I had my first lesson a few days later when about twenty of us were bundled into a truck and driven off into the mountains. We didn't know where we were going, or why, and I can remember looking out at the countryside, green and beautiful and apparently quite normal, with the natives strolling about leading their everyday lives, cars on the road, kids coming home from school. Nothing had happened, up to that point, to prepare us for what was to come.

The truck left the villages and the paddy fields behind and started to grind its way up into the mountains. After a quarter of an hour or so we stopped, and the Jap guards ordered us out of the lorries.

xi

Rumours, rumours, rumours: for three and a half years Bill and his fellow POWs had lived in the hope that the more optimistic ones might be true. American carrier battles, the reconquest of this island and that, the murderous advance of the "Forgotten Army" in Burma, the Second Front in Europe, VE Day — news of these events, vague, fragmentary, never quite confirmed, picked up by clandestine radios, or a chance remark by the guards, seeped into the camps, but there nothing changed except that the food became even more meagre, conditions even more unendurable. Finally, Bill says, "We got to the stage of not believing anything at all."

The effect on him, and on many other POWs, was a deep and abiding feeling of insecurity that fed and grew fat on the insecurity of their daily lives. For Bill above all, in his sightless, helpless state, it persisted, like his fear of being shut in, for years. Would this nightmare ever end — and what would become of him if and when it did?

Some time in 1945, four airmen who had been shot down were brought into the camp. They were the first reliable witnesses of what had been happening in the world outside during the last three years, and the tale they told sent a ripple of hope through the ever-sceptical ranks of the POWs. General MacArthur had returned to the Philippines, American and British carrier fleets were roaming at will off the Japanese mainland, despite the desperate onslaught of kamikaze aircraft. Tokyo was being regularly bombed by the Flying Fortresses of the US Air Force. Invasion of Malaya, and of Japan itself, seemed imminent. Surely the end of the Pacific War must be near?

The first atom bomb was dropped on Hiroshima on 6 August, the second, on Nagasaki, a couple of days later. Rumours of these events reached the camp during the ensuing week, followed by further rumours of an unconditional Japanese surrender. But would those in the outlying conquered territories accept it, or would they continue fighting, having, in all probability, massacred their prisoners first? Nobody could predict their reaction, and tension in all the camps, in Java, in Burma, in Japan itself, increased. In some, the Japanese guards and the loathed and feared kempei-tai sank to even lower levels of savagery, but the worst prophecies were mercifully unfulfilled.

Bill was sitting on his "bed" — the board, he says, which had served him for a bed for the previous six months, and which had had to be taken out and fumigated in the homemade incinerator in the camp grounds from time to time to get rid of the bugs — when he was aware of a sudden commotion in the room, but a commotion which was quite different from the usual ranting and bawling and sword-rattling that accompanied a visit by the camp commander and his guards. This time it was not the Japanese officer who was leading the procession, with the Allied officers behind, but the other way round, and when Colonel Peter Maisey reached Bill's bed he stopped, tapped him on the shoulder, and said, "Well, Billy, we've made it, haven't we?" And Bill realized that, at long last, the war was really over. Pride and wonder that at long last the war was over was mingled with a great sadness that so many had died, joy for those of us who had made it. When now they commemorate VE-Day on 6 June each year Bill thinks particularly of those who died between the ending of the European War and VJ-Day, two months later.

xii

The initial surge of relief and joy was followed by a sense of anti-climax, for life in the camp didn't seem, for the first week or so, to be very different from what it had been before. The food improved, certainly, though they were warned to be wary of eating too much after the years of eating too little. Then loudspeakers were rigged, and they all gathered round to listen to the World Service of the BBC, the sudden, almost unbeliev-able familiarity of a recognized voice saying, "This is the news and this is Bruce Belfrage reading it". The half-forgotten voice of the world beyond the wire, its music and its songs. The first one he heard, Bill remembers, was a popular little ditty, "Let's turn out the light and go to bed" — and the words had a certain poignancy in a place where bed was a board, and more than one listener was not to know whether the lights were on or not.

Information about Bill's injuries had been sent to the Air Ministry, and they had referred it to St

Dunstan's, the organization set up by the blind newspaper proprietor, Sir Arthur Pearson, in 1915, to rehabilitate servicemen blinded during the First World War. The Chairman, Lord Fraser, arranged for a telegram of encouragement to be sent to Bill, and he received it while he was still in Cycle Camp waiting to be sent home. It read:

"I lost my sight and hands in 1943 whilst serving with the 8th Army in North Africa. Having wonderful time at Dunstan's, learning to type and play the trombone, listening to radio, etc. Lots of friends here. Look forward to meeting. (Signed) David Bell."

There was no doubting the thoughtfulness of that gesture of solidarity, but for Bill it was double-edged. While he fully appreciated the message and its intention, it swung his mind towards a future which he feared and could not rightly imagine. What would be the reaction of his family and friends — pity, gradually eroding into impatience as they realized the extent of his dependence? And what about his wife, and the baby daughter whom he had left and who would now be four years old, and of whom he had thought so rarely during his captivity? How would they take it? Would there be some niche he could fill in the family business? If St Dunstan's could teach him to type, might he not find something to do in the office?

Confused by such a welter of unanswerable questions, such a tangle of anxieties and emotions, Bill found it difficult to join in the general rejoicing. "I had to make a great effort to appreciate the fact that the war was over," he wrote, "and that, although we were still in prison camp, we were free men again. Yet I desperately wanted to make the most of it and share the excitement with all the friends who had helped me weather those awful years as a POW."

xiii

Bill's first contact with that outside world was both comic and mildly macabre. He and his blind chum Ossy Gannon were summoned to go and talk to a number of reporters who were gathered just outside the camp. "We spruced ourselves up as best we could," Bill writes, "which wasn't very much, for I was still in my old shorts, bush-hat and flip-flops, though there was one improvement. I had, thanks to one of my fellow-prisoners, some improved artificial hands which he had made out of odd bits and pieces, a couple of old lampshades, some scraps of wire and goodness knows what else. Somehow he had managed to colour them to something resembling flesh, and they were attached to my arms with the elastic from a pair of pyjamas. In view of what happened, they must have been pretty realistic."

Bill and Ossy walked out of the camp arm in arm — quite something in itself, after three and a half years (not counting the time when Bill had found himself wandering out by mistake!) — and were at once assailed with questions, and with good news. Weary Dunlop, after two and a half years on the appalling Burma-Thailand railway, had survived, and sent good wishes and hoped they would soon meet again, if not in Java, then in England or Australia. Questions followed: how had they managed, how had the Japs treated them, were they looking forward to getting home, and so forth. Then, when the interviews were over, one of the reporters shook Bill vigorously by the hand — whereupon it came off! What's more, in the confusion, he never got it back, and no doubt one newsman went home with a good story — and a spare hand.

After a few minutes we walked back into camp. We didn't feel much different, and there weren't many outward signs of excitement or hilarity amongst any of us. I suppose our resistance was low, and we simply didn't have the emotional energy to respond to the change in our fortunes. It was a bit like being in a state of shock. I know all I wanted was to be alone, to try and take it in. I went back to my bed and lay there while my mind tried to focus on the future. Somewhere within me I knew that, during these years as a prisoner, I had been in a sense sheltered from reality. In our fenced-in world I had had friends and colleagues round me who were basically all in the same boat with me, and who were there, and were only too willing to help when help was needed. In the wide world outside I knew things would be very different, but it was a difference I could only vaguely imagine and wasn't much looking forward to.

The truth of it was I was scared stiff, and the closer that unknown future loomed, the worse it looked. After some time, I don't know how long, I and a number of the others were moved to a school which had been converted into an emergency reception centre. It was a considerable improvement on the camp, with comfortable beds, decent food, and the radio to listen to. We weren't allowed out as there were said to be a number of Japanese on the rampage close to the school; and I don't recall meeting any non-POW servicemen or civilians while I was there. It was like a kind of limbo, and I passed the time listening to the radio and occasionally wandering about the grounds with Ossy — the blind leading the blind!

At last the day came for us to leave Java. A hundred or so were taken to the airport and put on board a Dakota to be flown to Singapore. Six hours later we landed at Kallang, the very aerodrome I'd been stationed at four years before. The wheel had come full circle; but I couldn't help reflecting sadly that I was a very different person now from the carefree, adventurous lad who had arrived, all agog, in the *Cape Town Castle*. If only I had a little sight, or even a couple of fingers. Then I couldn't wait to savour the sights and smells of this vivid new world: now, when a friend persuaded me to accompany him into the city, I went reluctantly, and could hardly wait to get back to the hospital, to my bed, and to my great solace, the radio.

Not until long afterwards did I hear of the efforts made by St Dunstan's to trace blind POWs, efforts which were frustrated by the callous attitude of the Japanese towards us. In a recent letter, the Secretary of St Dunstan's, Mr William Weisblatt, says, "It was much later in the war" — after 1942, that is — "before we knew of any individuals who had lost their sight, and the records show that in January 1945 we arranged to send crates of supplies via the International Red Cross to two particular men of whom we had news. One was described as "A.C.1 William Griffiths" . . . As late as October, 1945, we only knew that four blind POWs had reached safety, and we were particularly concerned that we had no news of the chap in Java." In *St Dunstan's Review* for that month there was a note: "Unfortunately there is as yet no further news of the handless man who, when we last heard, was at a camp in Java."[1] In fact, the things they sent — they included books, a kit for making artificial arms, and a "mouthorgan adapted for handless use" — never reached us. We did, however, receive one small Red Cross parcel — shared between four of us — once the Japs had surrendered.

---

[1] Incredibly, in 1942, it was stated in Parliament that the number of prisoners of war in the Far Eastern Theatre was 3500! Actually there were 50,000 British alone.

No one who survived a Japanese POW camp
emerged physically fit, and Bill was no exception.
His injuries tend to disguise the fact in the telling, and undoubtedly his formidable constitution
enabled him to survive disease and malnutrition,
as well as his devastating disablement, better than
many, but he was less than half his proper
weight, and both physically and psychologically
undermined.

It was there, in Singapore, that the reality of my
situation hit me with full force, and I suddenly saw that
life was going to be very much harsher than I had led
myself to believe in the camps. Like every other POW I
longed for our captivity to be over, and although I knew
that nothing would ever give me back my sight or my
hands, yet I'd managed to persuade myself that,
somehow, once I was home again, life would be all
right. I should be fitted with artificial hands, and even
though I would always be blind, plenty of blind people,
as Andrew Crighton had said, succeeded in leading full
and useful lives. There would be friends and relations to
describe and explain things to me, just as my friends in
the camps did, and gradually I should be able to settle
down and work for the old firm. That was the dream
that had consoled me and helped me to keep going; but
now, in a new and strange and, as it felt to me, limitless
environment, I was no longer so sure. How *was* I going
to cope now the camp gates had opened and I was back

in the great big outside world? The doubts and fears nagged away at my mind, but I kept them to myself and did my best to join with the others in the pleasure of being free.

On arrival in Singapore we were taken to the hospital for a general check-up. There were a lot of RAF men there, and they did their best to cheer me up by painting a rosy picture of the future before me, and I pretended to believe them. Then Lady Mountbatten herself came to see me. She knew Lancashire, for her father had been MP for Blackpool, and she'd gone to the trouble to read my medical report. Like everyone else she sounded most encouraging. The RAF authorities, the Ministry of Pensions and St Dunstan's knew all about me, and I would be given top priority when it came to artificial limbs, training, and so forth. She even promised to come and see me in Blackburn, and I'm sure she meant it, but she died before she could make it. She was very practical and sympathetic and nice, and because I felt she was in a position to know what was possible and even do something about it, her visit gave me a much-needed boost.

Like the morphia which Mickey de Jonge used to give me during the worst times at the beginning, though, the effect didn't last. I felt confused and utterly weary, as if the heart had gone out of me. And when we began to hear details of the atrocities committed by the Japanese, including the appalling massacre by drunken guards of nurses and patients in this very hospital, sadness at the carnage and brutality and waste of it all became all mixed up with relief that it was over, and the apprehension over my own future, the conflict of emotions became too much to bear, and I would take refuge on my bed, listen to the radio, and try and forget all about it. One thing I could enjoy with no mixed feelings at all, however, was the food! Three square meals a day after those years of rice and seaweed were really something.

XV

After a week in Singapore a whole bunch of us was taken down to the docks and put on board the hospital ship *Somersetshire*, and so began, at last, the long journey home. And a long, slow journey it turned out to be. I don't remember that we were ever told the route we were to take, and we didn't even know until the night before we left whether we were going by sea or air. I can remember now the strange feeling of going up the ship's gangway, with all its associations with travelling out in the *Cape Town Castle*. Was all my life from now on to be nothing more than remembering the past and what it was like before?

I had the free run of the ship if I wanted it. We had been issued with RAF kit, and a dressing-gown — red, white and blue, I was told — which I had for years after; we even got some pay, and I was able to stock up with things that were supposed to be scarce at home — soap, chocolate, cigarettes — and I was faced with a new problem, handling money. That was one thing that I hadn't had to bother with in POW camp; but how do you handle money when you haven't any hands?

Answer: you don't. You rely on other people, and, being by nature an independent kind of bloke, this dependence on others really got me down. Just to be able to do *something* for myself! It's difficult to explain the contradictory feelings I had at this time. It was a bit like the story about the family on the beach at Blackpool and somebody asks the mum whether she's happy. "We're not happy and we're not unhappy, we're on 'us 'olidays". That's how it was with me: if anybody had asked me, I wouldn't have known what to say. I wasn't happy, and I wasn't unhappy, I wasn't even me. I didn't know what I was.

We crossed the Bay of Bengal and put into Madras, and there we had to leave the ship. Another move into the unknown. A military band played us ashore, and the local people all turned out to wave as we were shepherded into buses and on to the hospital train that was to take us to our next stopping-place, which I think was Poona. I know it took two days to cross India and as we trundled along various pals would try and describe the passing landscape for my benefit, which was good of them — but it wasn't the same as seeing it for myself. How could it be? I wanted to see this strange country and get the full impact of its strangeness.

Looking back now, I can see that it was the adjustments one had to make that were so difficult. In POW camp one was simply trying to survive. Life was grim, but there was no feeling that one was missing something, because there was nothing to miss. Not so now. There was a world of new experiences out there, beyond the carriage windows, to be gazed at and grasped and explored while I was trapped within my disabilities like a ferret in a sack. Many years were to pass before I learnt that there *is* an alternative way of life for disabled people, however severe their deprivation. Even being blind is not the end of the world.

From Poona — if it was Poona, one hospital's much like another! — we went by train to Bombay and on board another hospital ship, this time to take us up the Red Sea, through the Suez Canal — no going all the way round Africa on this voyage, for the war was really over — through the Mediterranean and home.

xvi

Home. More and more, as it drew daily nearer, my thoughts turned in that direction, and they were not all pleasant. Soon after we had boarded the *Somersetshire* in Singapore I received a letter, the first for nearly four years — and, of course, somebody had to read it to me. Letters, like money, had not been one of my problems in camp. It was a strange letter, and rather unsettling. In the first place, it was from my uncle, my father's brother, which was odd. He had taken over the family business when my father died — at the age of 40 — before the war, so he was the senior member of the family. But why had my mother not written? Was she too upset to write? Or perhaps she couldn't bear the thought of my coming home in this condition.

It was a cold letter. There was nothing about the business, nothing about my wife — presumably if she was ill or had died they would have mentioned it — nothing about my mother, except that she would be looking after me when I got home, at least for a while, although it would be hard for her — and when he knew where the ship was due to dock, he would meet me. And that was about all. Hardly the sort of letter to make a chap feel he was going to be very welcome when he got home. But worse than that, I had the feeling that a lot of things were being kept from me, things my uncle knew I shouldn't like. What were they? I'd had the whole two-month journey to brood about it, and although I tried not to worry too much, the unanswered questions would surface from time to time and increase my anxiety.

It must sound rather heartless, but the one thing I didn't worry about was my marriage. That was an incident which had happened to someone else, to Aircraftman First Class William Griffiths, RAF Transport Driver, twenty-one years old and in full possession of his faculties. Since she hadn't been mentioned, and there was no letter from her, I assumed she must have drifted off and found somebody else, as was common enough. Perhaps secretly I was a bit relieved. It would be perfectly understandable if she didn't want a wreck like me for a husband, and, if so, I'd rather not know. I had plenty of other things to worry about.

Once through the Straits of Gibraltar and heading north the weather started to grow colder, and the sea rougher. We were into November and the start of a grey, damp, cold English winter, quite a shock after four years in a tropical climate. I didn't need anyone to tell me what that looked like; and we arrived in the Mersey in fog. We stood shivering at the rail, and I could hear the others saying it was as thick as a hedge and they couldn't see a thing, which put us all in the same boat in more ways than one. I could hear ships hooting, voices shouting from ship to shore, the rumble as the engines went astern, all the excitement and bustle of coming alongside. We were home.

xvii

Someone collected my kit and escorted me down the gangway. At the dockside an ambulance was waiting and I was taken across to it, and I heard my uncle's voice.

"Billy! It's your Uncle Robert. How are you, lad?"

"Not too bad, Uncle," I said. There was a pause. The ambulancemen were fussing round, putting my kit on board, wanting to be off.

"They're taking you to the RAF Hospital at Cosford. I'll come along with you." There was another pause. "You don't look too bad at all," he said. "A bit older, perhaps, and a lot thinner."

"I expect I do."

"It's been a long time," my uncle said, and we clambered aboard. We were both embarrassed and awkward with each other, and although it was nice of him, I wished he hadn't bothered to come to meet me.

"How's mother?" I asked.

"She's fine."

"And the business?"

He hesitated for a fraction of a second, and then he said casually, "Oh, that's been sold up."

The bottom dropped out of what was left of my world.

CHAPTER
TWO

The Joys of
Homecoming

i

"In prison camp," Bill says, "we lived on dreams, and when my Uncle Robert told me the business was sold he destroyed my prison camp dreams in seconds. In seconds. For three and a half years I had clung on to the knowledge that, at least, there would be that to come back to, a haven in which, even though I should never be able to drive again, I would at least be able to be useful in the office, and get an occasional run on the old familiar routes as driver's mate. I was, after all, the eldest son, and had a right to take my late father's place — or so I'd imagined. It was a shattering blow.

When I'd recovered a bit, I managed to stammer out, "What happened? Why was it sold?"

My uncle muttered something about wartime difficulties, fuel rationing, the Ministry. Then he said,

"As a matter of fact, I've started up my own haulage business doing much the same kind of work as the old firm. It's going pretty well." And he changed the subject, going on, like they all did, about the generous pensions and allowances I should get and how I would be looked after and so on; but none of it made any sense to my numbed mind. The family business — sold! And here was he, my father's brother, running a similar business of his own. What had been going on while I was away?

"I have to tell you," Uncle Robert was saying, "Ethel, your wife, I'm afraid she's hooked up with someone else; had a baby by him, I hear. But your kid's OK. Ethel's sister's taken her on and she's doing fine. I daresay it's all for the best." He paused. "You'll be all right, lad, I'm sure of that. Your mother'll look after you; and there's St Dunstan's that cares for blinded servicemen, they'll help. You'll not be left to cope on your own."

I don't mind telling you, that ambulance ride to Cosford was one of the worst journeys in my life — second only to the drive to that other hospital in Java in the back of the army lorry after the explosion — and I was bloody glad when we arrived. Uncle Robert gave me a pat on the shoulder and buggered off back to Blackburn and *his* haulage business as quick as he could go, leaving me in the hands of a couple of WAAF nurses and an orderly who undressed me and whipped me into bed as if I was some kind of an invalid. I had the feeling that they were all wearing masks, as if I had the plague or something. Perhaps that's just what I had got — the plague of total disability. And as I lay there, in a strange ward in a strange hospital, with only the wireless — my familiar spirit — for company, I wondered what further blows fate had in store for me. They weren't long coming.

ii

"Come along, Billy! Time you were up and dressed! Your mother will be here directly." She and my two younger brothers were coming over from Blackburn. I hadn't seen them for over four years — and they hadn't seen me; and although I was eager to be with them, I was dreading it too, and my nerves, as I was led through to the waiting room, were really jangling. My brothers would be all right, but my mother. Would she burst into tears, or faint? Or scream? *I* didn't know what I looked like — Frankenstein's monster, for all I knew. "You're lucky," that Aussie had said to me in prison camp, "you can't see yourself."

"Billy!" There I was among them, their voices all round me. My mother was hugging and kissing me, and my brothers were putting their arms round me, and I heard mother say, with a kind of sob, "You're so thin, Billy," as if the first thing she wanted to do was get a good feed into me; and it was all right. A moment of intense, suppressed emotion, then Alan, my younger brother, put a cigarette between my lips and lit it for me, and we sat around smoking and talking.

They wanted to know all about prison camp, and the journey home, and mother kept on asking, "Are you really all right, Billy?" as if she couldn't quite believe it; and then we discussed when I should come home and who would come and fetch me, practical matters, and

65

the danger was past. We all went for a stroll in the grounds, and Robert and Alan took turns piloting me and we had a laugh, and then it was time for them, like any other visitors, to leave. And just like any other visitors and the relatives they had come to see, we said our goodbyes as if everything was normal, and when I was discharged I should be issued with a travel warrant and jump on a train — only we all knew that it wasn't like that and never would be.

Then came the shock. I've no idea what was said to mother when I wasn't there, but later that day, when I was back in the ward, someone — one of the orderlies, probably — came to my bed and said, quite abruptly, "Griffiths: your mother says she won't be able to look after you." Just like that, then went off before I could even ask him what he meant or how he knew. I sat there fuming, not only at the brusque way he'd said it, but — if it were true — the horror stories they must have told her about looking after a disabled son. Far from giving her some comfort and encouragement — and it didn't take much imagination to realize she must have been in a state of shock — it looked as if "they", whoever they were, had gone out of their way to emphasize the enormity of the task. It cheered me up no end, that did.

Then my brother Robert, who was still in the Royal Navy but had been granted six months' compassionate leave to help me, but was, in fact, working for Uncle Robert, promised to come for the weekend to see me, and that was something to look forward to. I was all keyed up for our reunion; but the day before he was due he phoned up the Hospital to say he couldn't make it as he was working. He'd come when he could. That was a double blow; not merely the disappointment of his not coming, but the reason for it: he was doing the job I'd hoped to have been doing before this lot happened; driving, the job I'd loved and would never be able to do again. The blind can learn many skills, but lorry-driving isn't one of them! It did teach me one lesson, though, and that was that I couldn't expect everyone to give up what they were doing and run around after me. They had their own lives to lead, and there wasn't much room in those lives for a dead weight like me.

I worried away at the orderly's remark about mother not being able to look after me. Was it true? And how could I find out? I couldn't use the telephone, and didn't feel like questioning the nurses about it. And if it was true, and she really felt it was too much for her, what was to become of me? Was I going to have to spend the rest of my life in some institution, like a criminal or a lunatic?

For the moment, though, the doctors and specialists hadn't finished with me. I was poked and prodded and examined and tested, and at the end of it they all came to the same conclusion, that, apart from the missing bits of me, and being underweight, like all FEPOWs[1], and therefore suffering from a certain debility, I was pretty fit, and all that was needed was time. When fully fit once more, I should be ready to take up some useful occupation. Such as what?

---

[1] Far East Prisoners of War

If there was no ready answer to that, perhaps my next port of call would supply one. In the C.O.'s car, and in the company of two extremely pleasant (pretty? — how should I know, and it didn't matter to me any more) WAAFs, one of them a nurse, I was taken in style to the artificial limb centre at Chapel Allerton, near Leeds. As it turned out, the best part of this jaunt was the journey itself, for we stopped for lunch on the way, and the two girls made me feel very much at ease. But so many people, in prison camp and afterwards, had assured me that once I was home I should be fitted with mechanical hands which could do anything, and I should be almost as good as new, that I was in a high old state of nervous anticipation.

The girls left me there — the job was apparently going to take three days — and by talking to the others who were there for the same reason, I soon discovered I was in good company. We were all ex-service — though I was the only blind one — and what a crew! One leg missing, two legs missing, one arm, two arms, or a mixture of these: it would have been quite comical if it hadn't been so grim, for all of us were going to have to cope with life under some form of disadvantage — and the authorities weren't so concerned with the problems of the disabled then as they have become since. But they were a cheerful lot and, perhaps because none of them had been in Japanese hands, they seemed a lot brisker and healthier than I did. My moods seemed to go up and down like a switchback, only much more down than up, and there was something about Chapel Allerton which got me right down. A chap with one leg even took five bob off me to join the British Limbless Ex-Servicemen's Association, which seemed a bit like adding insult to injury. Five shillings was a lot of money to me then, but Blesma is a wonderful organization and I have never regretted my contribution.

My first night there was horrible. I was terribly nervous and strung up and couldn't sleep, and if it hadn't been for my limbless colleagues, and a friendly night nurse who kept on bringing me cups of tea — which, of course, I couldn't hold, but tomorrow? — I should have been a wreck in the morning when I was due to be "fitted". This, I found, consisted of sitting for hours in what seemed to me more like a bus station than a waiting-room, with hundreds of adults and kids milling about, until a peremptory voice called out, "Griffiths, you can come in now", and I was led into the fitting-room and sat down on a chair. And sat, and sat, and black depression settled on me. It was like being told that the business had been sold; nobody cared or understood just how bloody awful it was to be blind and helpless and hustled about like a broken toy that needed mending.

At last the technician came over and took off my jacket and examined my stumps. "Whoever tidied these up made a decent job of it," he said, with professional interest.

"His name's Weary Dunlop," I said. "If it hadn't been for him, either I'd be dead, or you'd be fitting me with a tin leg as well."

But whatever interest he'd shown had evaporated. "Let's have a look."

69

He tried several pairs of arms on me. They appeared to be attached to a kind of harness made of leather and webbing that slipped over my shoulders, with hands and gauntlets socketed over my stumps. They felt very heavy and the only moving part was the thumb, which flicked in and out an inch or two. As far as I could tell they weren't any improvement on the tin cans and lampshades and bits of wire I'd had in prison camp, but he seemed satisfied.

"There you are," he said, "they're fine. They'll take a bit of getting used to, but once you get the hang of it, there's a box of gadgets that go with them, and you'll find you'll be able to manage quite well." He tucked the box under my arm and steered me to the door. "Right. Next!" And that was that. I had two hands that weighed a ton and which had a thumb each which moved rather less than a crab's claw — and, of course, a box of assorted gadgets. I was as good as new.

The crab's claws were disappointment number four.[1] They looked all right, my mother said, when, after my visit to Chapel Allerton, I was taken home to Blackburn; but when she saw how limited the movement was, and how little I should be able to do with them, I could feel the bitterness and disappointment welling up in her. There weren't going to be any

-----

[1] A lighter, more comfortable version has since been developed by Roehampton Limb Fitting Centre. Dr Fletcher and his associates have given constant practical help and advice over the past 28 years.

70

miracles after all, and she was going to be landed with a useless cripple. She didn't say as much, but I could read it in her voice. Perhaps that blasted orderly had been right, and she really couldn't cope with me.

This, remember, was my homecoming, the event I'd been looking forward to for nearly five years, first with longing, then with longing mixed with apprehension; for what I'd really been longing for was to come back as I had left, a little older, perhaps a little wiser, but essentially the same old Billy of William Griffiths (Blackburn) Ltd. And that was not to be.

Relatives and friends came to visit — friendly, sympathetic, trying their level best to behave as if nothing had changed. Was I being over-sensitive to feel a bit like a freak in a sideshow? "Walk up, walk up, and see the eyeless, handless man!" No, that's unfair, but I did, sometimes, feel an object of pity, yes, and curiosity. How people behave towards the disabled is often, I think, a test of their maturity, and I should know! Perhaps it's only a form of shyness, I'm sure it is, but it's not very nice for the recipient who wants nothing more in the world than to be normal and, failing that, to be treated as if he — or she — were. Never mind. It was lovely to hear their familiar voices and to know that, however different "home" was from what I'd imagined and dreamed about for all those years, it was still home. Here, though I couldn't see them, were the streets and mills that I'd known all my boyhood; this was where I belonged.

Part of that life had been my wife, Ethel, and, on one of the two days I was at home, her sister and her husband came to see me. That was a bit awkward, too, to begin with, but it worked out all right.

"We're ever so sorry," Ada said, "you had to come back and find Ethel had — er — gone off with someone else. It's too bad. But Eileen's a lovely little girl, and we're so happy looking after her." She paused, and then said, "In fact, if it was possible, we'd like to keep her. Wouldn't we, Alf?"

"We would that," said Alf.

"Not having any of our own," Ada said. "You know."

"It's very good of you both," I said. "Let's discuss it later, when I've settled down."

"Yes, of course, later," they said eagerly. "It's too soon. When you've only just come home. We'll discuss it later."

I certainly couldn't look after the child, and if that was what they wanted it seemed an ideal solution and I'd happily go along with it. It was just another bit of the past that had gone missing.

iii

At the end of the two days my two WAAFs arrived to take me back to Cosford — but not for long. I'd just about settled down there once more when I was summoned to the consulting room where my eye sockets were to be examined by none other than Sir Archibald MacIndoe. He was the surgeon who had performed miracles of plastic surgery on burn cases, notably RAF aircrew. He was kindness itself and, after the examination, he explained that it would be possible for me to wear glass eyes, which would improve my appearance, but I would have to have an operation on the sockets because, over the years that had elapsed since I was blinded, the lids had closed over them. It wasn't a big operation, but it would mean being admitted to Stoke Mandeville Hospital.

"That's fine," I said, but inwardly I just shrugged. I'd begun to realize that I was no longer my own master but a kind of robot, to be despatched hither and yon at the discretion of others. They had the controls, not I. You may think that after four years I should have grasped that; but I'm a stubborn so-and-so, and I went on fighting the dependence that had been imposed on me. I still do. But this time, at least, there wouldn't be any disappointment involved, as there had been over the hands. Glass eyes might make me look more human, but no one had ever suggested that they might enable me to see again!

So it was off again; another round of goodbyes to staff and my fellow-patients, and another place to try and get the measure of. It seemed to have happened so often during those years. It was also virtually goodbye to the RAF, although technically I was still a member of the Service since I hadn't been demobbed. From then on I had little or no contact with them, though I wasn't actually back in civvy street till the April of the following year, 1947.

iv

At Stoke Mandeville I entered, for the first time, the world of the blind, for St Dunstan's had a unit there, and I came into contact with the organization which was to play a vital role in my life during the years ahead. The main thing at this time was that all of us in the unit were blind, and that made all the difference. Better still, one of them — the only other FEPOW — was my old pal, Ossy Gannon. Another was a lad from Salford by the name of Arthur Cavanagh, who, in addition to being blind, had also lost both his hands, but in North Africa. Despite this, he was astonishingly cheerful, and the way he had come to terms with it was a lesson to me. He had also been issued with the crab's claws and found them totally useless, so that was a comfort — of a kind. At least it disposed of any false hopes I might have had and enabled me to realize that it wasn't just me.

I've often heard people ask the question, which is worse, to be blind or deaf? Unless you've known blindness and deafness separately, there's no way of telling, though most would say blindness was the worst of all. With us at Stoke Mandeville it didn't arise and the additional disabilities that some of us had were just something we had to accept. Arthur and I were equal, so to speak. Another bloke, Ron Slade, had lost one hand and part of the other, but he was also partially deaf, and had lost all sense of taste and smell. He would ask Arthur what was for dinner and whether it was good or not. If Arthur said it was all right he'd enjoy it; but if he said it was horrible Ron used to think so too! Yet, for all that, he was wonderfully cheerful and we had a lot of laughs together. Neither of them had a trace of self-pity, and this made a great impression on me. I'd tried to avoid it in prison camp and although there were obviously times then, and there would be more in the years ahead, when it would have been easy to give way to it, I was determined not to if I could help it. Thinking about men like Arthur and my other handless friends helped a lot; if they were able to keep their spirits up in spite of everything I should be able to do the same. But there was a difference. They had not been in Jap hands, and often in those days I felt as if the stuffing had been knocked out of me.

Once the operation on my eye sockets was completed and the wounds had healed, which wasn't long, I was able to join in the various social activities which the members of St Dunstan's staff organized. There were dances with local girls invited in as partners, occasional trips to Aylesbury or one of the local pubs for a good old-fashioned sing-song. Arthur rather fancied himself as a singer — I can still hear him warbling his favourite, "Shine Through My Dreams" — and was a bit of a comic as well. Anything for a laugh.

St Dunstan's main home for those blinded on war service was at Ovingdean, near Brighton. This magnificent building — which I was to come to know very well later on — had only been finished the year before the start of the Second World War, and was taken over by the Navy and, in the peculiar way the Navy has of naming buildings as if they were ships, became HMS *Vernon*. St Dunstan's itself had moved out of the danger area to Church Stretton in Shropshire, where it occupied a number of hotels, with a small separate unit at Stoke Mandeville, where I was. Soon after Christmas, 1945 — my first in England for five years — this unit was to be closed down and the patients transferred temporarily to Church Stretton until Ovingdean was ready for reoccupation. As this was due to happen early in the New Year, and I'd been away so long, I was asked if I would rather go home, and I agreed.

It was difficult at this time to know *what* I wanted to do. Obviously I did want to go home, even though it wasn't the home I'd been looking forward to, and I wasn't quite the prodigal son. At the same time I'd come to appreciate the comradeship of other blind and disabled people. I suppose it's a case of "birds of a feather . . ."; in each other's company, and under the wing of an organization which understood our difficulties and limitations, we weren't objects of curiosity or pity, and we didn't feel we were a burden to anyone. Particularly in these early days this fellowship in misfortune helped tremendously in building up confidence and the strength to face the future. Later on I was to realize that it had its dangers too.

Anyway, the decision was made, my few belongings were packed, I was allocated an escort and taken by train back to Blackburn to celebrate this first peacetime Christmas with my family.

★   ★   ★

While I'd been away, my mother had remarried. She was now Agnes Walmsley. Her husband, William, was a watchmaker by trade, a pleasant, patient, easy-going sort, and we got on very well. He did a lot of his work at home and I could imagine him with his watchmaker's glass in his eye poring over the tiny springs and cogs and jewels he was busy reassembling. I'd not known him before, so he was only a presence and a voice. I'd sit quietly in a corner of his workroom; we'd exchange the odd word; then I'd hear him push back his chair and get up and he'd say, "Well, Billy, what about a walk?" He would help me into my coat and take my arm and we'd potter off together to the local park. He never seemed to mind or make me feel it was a chore for him. He'd tell me about the changes that had taken place in the town and about people we both knew. Blackburn, the working part that we belonged to, was a very close community in those days. Everybody knew everybody else — and everybody else's business as well!

My paternal grandfather was still alive, though he'd retired from the business, which he had started, some years before. He too — it makes me sound like a Labrador or something — would come over once or twice a week and take me out for a walk. I enjoyed that, for, like me, he knew every road and street in the town, and I could picture in my mind the exact route we were taking and the buildings that lined them. It would've been even better to see them for myself — but there we are.

Grandpa had started out in the fruit and vegetable trade before going into haulage, and he'd often take me to the market in the centre of the town where he knew, and was known by, everyone, and, of course, they knew me too. We'd wander round behind the stalls for a chat and the owners would give me a tap on the shoulder, "Good to see you again, Billy," and tell us to help ourselves. One of them, who'd had a shop near where we lived when I was a youngster, said when we went to see him, "You know, Billy, I'd be a lot better off today if it hadn't been for you."

"How do you make that out?"

"What about all those apples and oranges you pinched off my stand, then?" he said, and roared with laughter. So he'd known about it all the time when us kids on the way back from school would nick something when we thought he wasn't looking! Our family were good customers of his, so he'd let us get away with it.

Grandpa had been born with a withered arm and this made him all the more sympathetic and understanding to me. "It hasn't made life any easier, having only one good arm," he said, "but I managed, and so will you." He was trying to encourage me, I knew, and, in fact, I did try and manage myself later on. At that time, however, I couldn't see the slightest hope of doing so.

It must have been all the more galling for him, therefore, to have the firm he'd created, and which he, my father and his brother had built up, gone, finished! So that now he had no power to give me a job in what was my uncle's business. More than once he said to me, "Oh Billy, you've come home too late," and there was sorrow and bitterness in his voice. They were feelings I could share. Whether it would have made any difference if I'd come home in one piece is another matter, but at the heart of it was the fact that no one had expected me to come home at all. I was the ghost at the banquet.

I felt this most at home. Alan, my youngest brother, had always been the baby of the family. He was six years younger than Robert, and, inevitably, mother's favourite. He was still living at home, and to find himself displaced from the centre of her attention, having had her to himself all those years, was not at all to his liking and mother wasn't a strong enough character to put him in his place. I had the feeling that they would both have been a lot happier if I wasn't around. Unintentionally, perhaps, they made me feel like an intruder, and that is not pleasant when you know there's absolutely nothing you can do about it.

For all that, life wasn't too bad. Cousin Edith wrote letters for me. Dad's sister-in-law, Aunt Emily, had three daughters, Emily, Doris and Gladys, about my own age, and they used to come round and take me out with them for the evening. I often stayed with them for the weekend, as well, which cheered me up as they were good company. "Grandma Griffiths", as we always called her, who was a very lively old lady, accepted my various disabilities philosophically and never minded helping me with meals or in the toilet. That generation was very down to earth; they'd had to be.

During this time I was also able to sort out the problem of my daughter, Eileen. Ethel's sister and her husband, who had no children of their own and had looked after her from the age of one, were keen to adopt her, indeed would have been heartbroken if they'd had to give her up. I could not look after her, so, after considerable thought, I agreed. It was a solution that pleased everyone. Later on Ethel and I were divorced, and Eileen took Ada and Alf's name.

What I needed above all was something useful, constructive, to do. I wanted to work and couldn't, could see no prospect of working, and the frustration of it really got me down. If mother had accepted the situation more readily I should have been less miserable, but she felt helpless in the face of it, for she was not of the type who can take such disasters in their stride and it began to affect her health. The situation, and the prospect ahead, were both pretty bleak; but help was on the way.

vi

I'd been at home for about six months when the local St Dunstan's Welfare Officer came to see me. She'd been before but this time it was to suggest that I should have a spell at Ovingdean, which was once more their Rehabilitation and Training Centre after the disruption caused by the war.

Should I go? I'd certainly felt happy with the St Dunstaners at Stoke Mandeville, but that was just a small unit, informal and friendly. Those words,

"Rehabilitation", "Training Centre", had a different and less welcoming ring to them altogether. I foresaw some kind of institution with rules and regulations, and I'd had a bellyful of that in POW camps. Not that I imagined Ovingdean would be run by Jap guards, don't think that! I just felt I'd had enough of institutions of any kind, and I told her so.

"Give it a go," she said. "If you really can't stand it after a week, they'll bring you back home."

That was something, but I still wasn't sure. It was the old thing — I simply didn't know what to do, because there didn't seem to be anything I could do. If someone offers you the choice between being shot or hanged, it doesn't seem to matter too much which you choose, the result will be the same either way. Whether I went or whether I stayed, it seemed to me, I should be the same useless wreck and a burden on whoever had to look after me.

"You got on so well with the St Dunstaners at SM," the Welfare Officer said, "and at Ovingdean you'll meet many others. I'm sure you'll enjoy it there."

Well, I wasn't enjoying things much in Blackburn, so in the end I allowed myself to be persuaded. Full marks to her for persistence; she knew what she was talking about, and I would soon learn.

That final fortnight before I went was pretty hectic. All the haulage contractors in Blackburn contributed a fiver to a collection for me. Others wanted to put on a benefit concert for me, but for some reason grandpa wouldn't allow it — his pride, I think. He couldn't accept the idea of his grandson being an object of charity. I had a visit from Ethel, my wife, in contrite mood, but the divorce was already in progress and I'd no inclination to change my mind. I preferred to be unattached. In contrast, I also had a visit from the Bishop of Blackburn, which, for a busy man, was kind, I thought. We chatted a bit about prison camp and how I'd coped, and then knelt and prayed together in the parlour. He had brought a gift from his wife, a quarter of a pound of potted meat which she had made. It doesn't sound much these days, but then, when meat and most other things were still rationed, it meant a lot more. It was a very friendly gesture.

When grandpa took me to the garage to say goodbye to one or two pals, and I mentioned the Bishop's visit and his gift, the mechanic let out a guffaw and shouted to the world at large, "What do you know! The Bishop's brought Billy some potted meat!" For some reason the idea of the Bishop arriving at our house with a little jar of potted meat absolutely knocked them over and they roared with laughter. When I tried to defend him by saying he meant well, it simply set them off again. Crude lot!

Then Uncle Robert insisted I make a will. As I only had about £150 in the world, my RAF back pay, I thought this was quite funny, but there was an ulterior motive. Grandma Griffiths had decided to leave me something, and they didn't want it to go to Ethel if I were to pop off before the divorce was made absolute. For various reasons I never got it; but it didn't matter, and in any case Grandma Griffiths lived on, happily for many years.

At last the time came for me to set off for Ovingdean. My brother Robert got time off to accompany me. I was wearing the "crab's claws" which, useless though they were, I had got used to, and I insisted on walking to the station, down the old familiar streets; not, I felt, for the last time, but because this did feel like a turning-point and I was sure that once I got to St Dunstan's I wasn't going to hurry back, however "institutional" it turned out to be. I had been disappointed so often since my return home. Was this to be just another disappointment, I wondered?

vii

The "institution" to which Bill Griffiths was bound that June of 1946 had been the achievement of one man, the newspaper proprietor Sir Arthur Pearson who had lost his own sight — through natural causes — in 1913. All too soon after that the first men blinded on the Western Front began to arrive in England, and Pearson, who was working for the National Institute for the Blind, decided to set up a hostel specificially for the war-blinded where he could put into practice his theories — commonplace now, revolutionary then — as to how blind people should be treated.

"I realize," he wrote, "that it is the blind man who, above all, needs occupation, and that the more active, the more normal he can make his life, the happier he will be . . . If you tell a man often enough that he is afflicted, he will become afflicted."

Anyone who has read Bill's story so far will recognize the fundamental truth of Pearson's words.

From a hostel in Bayswater to a borrowed mansion in Regent's Park, the organization grew with the need for it: to West — now Pearson — House in Brighton, and then to its own, purpose-built establishment — now known as Ian Fraser House — at Ovingdean. This last was Bill's destination.

It stands on sloping ground, a fold of the South Downs, looking for all the world like a rather posh hotel staring out over the sea and along the coast to Brighton, Worthing, Bognor Regis and Selsey Bill. They say you can even see the Isle of Wight on the clearest days — if, that is, you can see at all. From the main entrance paths radiate across the smooth downland turf to the sports ground, to the seashore and, via a subway under the main coastal road, to the bus stop; each path railed in on both sides so that the blind can navigate themselves round the grounds or into Brighton by way of the Undercliff walk, as many of the braver souls do. As soon as Robert told Billy about the railings Billy's spirits lifted; at least here he'd be able to wander about alone, something he hadn't been able to do since

POW camp, tapping round with his stick jammed into an old tin can.

They had been met at Brighton station by the hostel's own transport, and now Robert escorted Bill through the revolving door into the entrance hall.

"Ah, Mr Griffiths. Your room's on the third floor, number six. I'll get someone to take you up."

Those first impressions, the railings — indoors as well as out — the friendliness of the welcome, the atmosphere, efficient but informal, all helped to calm his apprehensions. This, Bill thought, is going to be all right. He said goodbye to Robert, who was going to stay in Brighton overnight before returning home to Blackburn and he was on his own, but, he was sure, in good hands. For a little while he stood chatting with the hall porter, who told him a bit more about the place.

"It's shaped rather like an aircraft," he said, "with the hall where we are now, and the stairs and landings forming the fuselage, and the lounges, the dining-room, and the bedrooms above, all in the two wings. In the centre, right in front where the engine would be, is the chapel."

For those able to make use of it, there was a large model of the building on a stand in the centre of the entrance hall, so designed that the lay-out could be "read" by touch, and a smaller, similar model gave the plan of the grounds in relation to the building, but neither of these was any help to Bill.

A nursing orderly came to lead him to his room on the third floor. He made Bill follow the handrails with his gloved, unfeeling paws and explained each turn as they came to it, and the swinging gates at the head of each flight of stairs. He was to share a room with a man by the name of Reg Page. The orderly unpacked his kit, helped him have a shower and get dressed, and then took him downstairs for his first communal meal.

When he'd first arrived Bill had been impressed with the quietness of the place. When he entered the dining-room he was amazed by the noise, for all eighty or so of Ovingdean's inhabitants were now gathered, ten to a table, for supper, and the hall was buzzing with conversation. Quite a contrast to those silent meals at home. Bill found himself with his Stoke Mandeville friends, and this immediately put him at his ease. Here he was, in a huge, strange room, surrounded by people whose faces he would never know, but with voices he could recognize, and problems similar to his own; and he could forget for a time the anxieties and frustrations that had so darkened his time at home, the vexations of idleness and dependence.

That evening his chum Arthur Cavanagh, blind and without hands like Bill, rounded him up to go with a bunch of the lads to the White Horse in Rottingdean for a few jars. A coach took them and would bring them back at closing time, and soon they were settled into the bar, a score of fellows, all blind, chatting away like any other customers, the fact that two of them, at least, could only have a drink if one of the staff who had come with them held their pints to their lips not detracting at all from the general merriment. Two of the company, semi-blind through malnutrition, had also been prisoners of the Japanese, and their presence increased Bill's sense of belonging, though no one mentioned the war or how he'd been wounded. "That," Bill says, "was of no consequence now. We were together, enjoying ourselves, discussing what we'd done that day and what we would be doing during the days ahead, adjusting to the realities of our situation. How we all came to be there was part of a past we none of us wanted to think about any more, which meant that we were taking the first steps towards coming to terms with reality."

Tucked up into bed by Andy, the orderly that night, a mug of Horlicks inside him, Bill found himself sleepless but with a new-found sense of contentment. Apart from the fact that the door had knobs, not levers, so that he couldn't let himself in or out, and the old fear of being trapped returned to haunt him, his introduction to St Dunstan's, with its care and thoughtfulness and easygoing routine, and the feeling of being among friends, had been a rare pleasure, and if, deep down inside him, he felt that nothing had really changed, or ever could change, he was prepared to ignore it. There would be plenty of time to worry about that in the weeks to come.

viii

St Dunstan's rare ability to heal the psychological wounds of being blinded was well described by another of the many who have found solace and a source of strength there. Wally Thomas was a corporal in a bomb disposal squad when he was blown up while dealing with a 2,200 lb German bomb, and left blind and deaf. In his book[1] he wrote of Ian Fraser House: "The view from those thousand windows is, I am told, unrivalled along the South Coast . . . It required a night's thought for me to decide that it was right that a house of blind men should enjoy these magnificent views that they would never see. Because we know they are there . . . We could as easily live in a dark building shut off by high walls in the hollow of the land, since we can see nothing wherever we are, but we would know we were there, and we would be less happy in such a place. We have walls of our own, and darkness, as it is." And he says, "When we sit on

[1] Life in My Hands, Heinemann, 1960

the terraces, we face the English Channel, and we know it. We can smell its clean tang and we can picture it just as it is. We couldn't do this unless it were really there."

When the physical eyes have gone, the mind's eye needs all the nourishment it can get, and when Bill, on his first full day there, walked to Rottingdean, escorted along the sea front, he was aware of the waves breaking on the beach, the cars on the main road, and tried to imagine the St Dunstan's building — like an ocean liner, Wally Thomas thought — up on the hill. Whether these mental pictures bore any relation to the reality was immaterial, for the reality that mattered was being able to memorize a route, not by its scenic attractions, which did not apply, but by all the small, apprehensible physical details.

When I'd mastered a general plan of the grounds and been to the two nearby villages of Ovingdean and Rottingdean on the arm of friends who were able to use a stick and knew the way, I decided it was time for me to be a little more adventurous. Not being able to carry a stick myself — a simple task quite beyond the useless crab's claws — was a major snag, but by making myself memorize every detail as I walked with my companions — the width of a path or pavement, what lay on either side of it, the necessary clues as to which way to turn and when — I gradually built up a complete mental picture of the various walks both inside and beyond the grounds.

For my first sortie on my own I set off — without telling anybody — downhill, following the rails, to the wicket gate that took one on to the pavement alongside the main coast road. I was able to open the gate; then, I knew, I had to turn left, and by walking with one foot on the pavement and the other on the grass verge, I could navigate safely to my destination. This, on this first exciting and rather tremulous solo expedition, was a lane that turned off to the left, towards Rottingdean. I'd been along it many times with my blind friends tapping their way along, but I wasn't going to risk taking it at this stage. I dared not, for the life of me; all I wanted to do was get to it and be certain that I'd done so.

Slowly I shuffled along, one foot on the path surface, the other on the grass, all the while keeping a mental check on the distance I'd travelled. Beside me I could hear the cars passing; when they passed the opening of the lane, the sound changed, and I knew I was getting close. Now I had to be careful, because the pavement ended and there would be a step down. There were people about, I could hear their footsteps and their voices as they turned into the lane or emerged from it. Ah! — that's it; my right foot registers the edge of the pavement; the lane is on my left. I've made it, my first journey alone outside the grounds. I turn round, right foot on the grass this time, back the way I had come. The only worry now was not to go past the wicket gate. Just past it there was a wire fence instead of the hedge, so I should know if I'd gone too far. Getting close I can feel the change of level; there's the gate now.

Triumphantly, I let myself in, and follow the railings back up the hill to the house. My first unescorted walk in the great wide world beyond the boundary fence — and no danger of wandering out of the main gate of the camp and being driven back by an indignant Jap sentry!

I tell no one. I hug the sense of achievement to myself. Tomorrow I shall do it again. I might even go further. I will gradually do every walk that is possible and not too dangerous without a stick. I do not want help or advice from anyone. That things will not always go so smoothly I am quite sure: the danger of collision, tripping over the odd step, missing a vital turning — these are regular hazards, and unavoidable, but nothing to the relief and pleasure of even this minute degree of independence.

On more ambitious sorties Bill often had for companion and guide a man by the name of Jack Palmer whose eyes had been damaged in the First World War, but who had a little sight. Arms linked, Bill, Jack and Arthur Cavanagh would set off with due caution, "Jack squinting his way along for us", for a stroll along Palace Pier, a jar at the British Legion Club, or a pint and a sandwich at the White Horse. On these expeditions Jack was often better at finding his way along the front than he was at finding Bill's mouth when it came to feeding him.

Bill found getting about outdoors much easier than indoors. He could form no clear plan of the building in his mind; and if he did find his way, say, from the lounge to his room, he was unable to open the door when he got there; so he had to call on someone to guide him. Later on, however, he came to know the building so well that the problem solved itself, and the doors were later fitted with lever handles.

Blind people, Sir Arthur Pearson determined, need an occupation, and to lead as normal and active a life as possible, and at Ian Fraser House the staff set out to follow this dictum to the letter. Patients, if that's the word, were encouraged to exercise all the freedom they were capable of, indoors and out, and to take part in as many sports and other activities as they could. Apart from vocational training, which was central to the St Dunstan's philosophy from the start, there were plenty of more frivolous occupations: visits to the theatre and cinema — though Bill never really recovered from his disappointment on going to a Laurel and Hardy film back in Blackburn and discovering how much of their humour depended on being able to see them — evenings out here and there, and even a day at the races.

"Following the gee-gees" was highly organized, slightly to Bill's surprise.

During breakfast I listened to the announcements and heard them say that "the stables" would be open at 9.15. Stables, I thought. Were they going to put us on the back of a horse next? I needn't have worried. "The

Stables" turned out to be one of the lounges which was given over to the racing enthusiasts. Here the Sports Officer sat at a desk with a pile of newspapers from which he read out all the information about the day's race meetings, the runners for each race, and the form, and the punters listened intently with hardly an interruption, just the odd query about weight or the starting price. Then, one by one, they went up to the desk to place their bets. I found their knowledge of the horses, and the way they were able to rattle off the names of their selections and their doubles and trebles absolutely amazing. I tried to keep up with them, but it was hopeless. These chaps were serious betting men, and I was an also-ran. All I could do was ask the Sports Officer to pick three horses for me from the tipsters, and get the cash out of my pocket for me. Once all the bets were on, they were taken round to the local bookmaker and, later, the punters would gather round the radio to listen to the race commentary. Whether I won or lost I can't remember now, though I dare say I would have remembered if I'd won.

Something far more important than betting on horses happened that first morning, though. I was in the lounge nattering with my handless friends Tommy Gaygan, Ted Miller and Dickie Brett when I felt a hand on my shoulder, and a quiet voice said, "Bill, Dacre here; will you come into my office for a chat?" This was my first meeting with Air Commodore G. B. Dacre, the C.O. of Ian Fraser House. In the friendliest way he took my arm and led me into his office and sat me down, and started talking about the after-effects which everyone suffered after having been a POW, especially when combined with the injuries I'd received. He himself had been a prisoner of the Turks during World War One, he said, and although they were nothing like as bad as the Japanese, they were not the gentlest of captors, so he had some idea of what I'd been through. The great thing was not to worry if I felt nervous and frustrated now that I was faced with the problems of adjusting to normal life. It was only to be expected, and St Dunstan's job was to make that transition as smooth as possible. Above all, there was no hurry. What I needed was time and rest, and only when I felt ready for the next stage need I start thinking about the future. I could stay as long as I liked, do as much or as little as I liked, and if I wanted to discuss any ideas I might have, I only had to come and see him.

This was exactly the kind of reassurance I needed, from someone who, I felt, knew what he was talking about, and I could have done with it much sooner after my return home. It was a real morale-booster and, when the interview was over and he took me back to the lounge, I felt as if a great weight had been taken off my mind. Blind and without hands I might be, but there was still a bit of life left. I could walk and talk and hear and enjoy the company of friends, and, who knows, I might still find something worth living for.

ix

I began by learning to play the trombone. The Research Department had produced a gadget which, when fitted to the body of the instrument, enabled me both to hold the mouthpiece to my lips and move the slide in and out. A couple of my handless friends were already learning the instrument and I joined them. The sound we produced may not have been music — Tommy Dorsay had nothing to worry about! — but eventually I was able to blow the odd little tune to my satisfaction, if to no one else's. The important thing, though, was to be doing something, learning something, and in the company of others equally ill-equipped to do so.

Far more valuable than tootling away on the trombone was learning to type. Although there have been improvements over the years, the principles haven't changed — the metal cover over the keys with a hole for each letter, and the striker attached to my stumps, as described earlier. It took me many months of patient practice to master, and some of my early efforts must have looked as if they'd been produced by a drunken chimpanzee, but I got it eventually and my speed and accuracy gradually improved. I can't say that, even now, when I do a certain amount of typing pretty well every day that I'd get a job as a secretary, but I realized right from the start that to be able to type would be a tremendous advantage, as well as giving me a precious measure of independence, so I persevered. It's a lot more useful than playing the trombone!

From time to time Air Commodore Dacre would call me into his office for a chat, to ask me how I was getting on, and on one of these occasions I happened to mention the family haulage business and how desperately I'd hoped to be able to take some part in it, but everything had changed in my absence and now there was no place for me. He didn't say anything for a moment or two, then he said quite casually.

"Ever thought of starting up on your own, Billy?"

"My own haulage business, you mean?"

"Why not?"

"Do you think I could — like this?"

"It's worth thinking about. If you're interested, leave it with me and I'll make some inquiries and let you know what I find out."

"Fine," I said. "Thank you."

I left him with my head fairly buzzing. Could I possibly manage it? Was it even possible? I was completely out of touch with conditions in the industry, though I did know that to get a licence to operate was by no means easy. Every application for an "A Licence" was automatically opposed by other hauliers, and by the railways, who resented the competition. But even supposing I could get over that hurdle, I'd have to buy a lorry — and I had no money. I'd have to employ a driver. Would Alan come in with me? But he couldn't drive. Would Robert leave his uncle and come and drive for me? The questions hammered away in my head, and with the questions came the old fears. I knew all too well what living at home was like, whereas here at St Dunstan's I was happy and relaxed, surrounded by friends, and by staff who were experienced and understanding. I had no worries. I could go my own pace, practise my typing and live on the dream that one day I might find something useful to do . . . one day.

As I tried to weigh up the pros and cons in my mind I regretted ever having mentioned the business to Air Commodore Dacre; yet at the same time I knew in my bones that if I didn't accept the challenge I should regret it for the rest of my life. It would be easy to settle gently into the pleasant, easy routine of Ian Fraser House, the permanent resident of a comfortable and undemanding institution, well-fed, well-looked after and completely useless. And that just wasn't good enough. I *had* to find out if I was capable of leading as normal a life as my disabilities allowed.

In any case I hadn't reckoned with St Dunstan's power of research and organization. The Air Commodore produced a man who was not only well-acquainted with the transport industry but who also knew all about business management and book-keeping, and I spent quite a number of brain-stretching hours under his tuition learning the basics of double entry, invoicing, health insurance conditions of employment, employers' liability and all the rest of it — matters which I'd hardly ever heard about during my carefree days as a mere driver. And it all had to be memorized; there was no question of a quick check in the book of words for me. I had to remember it, or ask someone. This same gent helped me to apply for a licence and put me in touch with certain people in Blackburn who agreed to support my application. In the end British Rail withdrew their opposition and it was granted.

There was still the vital question of a vehicle. I knew what I wanted, an 8-wheeler for which no second man was needed, but although St Dunstan's agreed to lend me the money, they were hard to find in 1946, and in the end I had to make do with a 4-wheeler and trailer, which — because, legally, a mate was obligatory — would reduce the margin of profitability considerably. In the meantime I put my new, but somewhat shaky, skill as a typist to the test and wrote to a number of contacts in Lancashire in the hope of acquiring a small, going business. Nothing came of it, but it was all good practice for the time when I would actually have a business of my own to manage. I also taught myself to use the telephone by dialling with my tongue, which sounds difficult — and is — but can be done if you happen to be short of fingers.

All this kept me busy as autumn gradually turned to winter, but there was still time to take part in the merry round of activities, to wander round the grounds following the handrails or amble off with Jack and Arthur for a drink at the White Horse. There was still time, too, to forget the whole thing, for I had not finally committed myself to leaving, and there were many occasions during those months when I felt severely tempted to abandon the idea, or at least to put it off. So often the difficulties seemed insuperable, not merely because of my own limitations but because everything was still upside down after the war, and, with the Labour Government in power, there were many uncertainties, particularly in the field of transport. In fact, it was probably about as bad a time to try and start a haulage business as can be imagined.

As the months went by I discovered that I had started something which I couldn't stop. I had the necessary rudimentary skills which would enable me to run the business, I had the finance to buy the vehicle, and my two brothers had agreed to come in with me as driver and mate. Finally there was no turning back, and I decided to leave Ovingdean and return home in time for Christmas. The night before, there was a big works dance in the neighbourhood and a bunch of us from Ian Fraser House was invited. There were plenty of girls to dance with, the beer flowed freely, and a good time was had by all. At the end of the evening one of my friends called for silence and announced that I would be leaving the following day. Whereupon the band struck up "For he's a jolly good fellow", everyone joined in, and I sat there like an idiot with the tears rolling down my cheeks. Yes, even without eyes you can still cry!

So this was it. People kept on coming up and patting me on the shoulder and wishing me good luck, and by the time we finally got into the transport to take us back I was a nervous wreck. To say I had cold feet would be the understatement of the year. What on earth had possessed me, I asked myself, to imagine I could start and run any kind of business, and why the hell was I leaving this cosy, comfortable life and all my pals when I didn't have to? And yet, even as I cursed myself for being utterly daft, I knew I had no choice. Right from the early days in POW camp I had brooded on what I should be able to do with my life. At that time all my hopes had been centred on the family firm. Back home, with that gone by the board, I had reached rock bottom once more. Now, with a bit of self-confidence restored, I had my chance.

Next morning, 19 December, 1946, I left St Dunstan's with my escort for Blackburn and the start of my great adventure.

CHAPTER
THREE

Back to Work

i

The frustrations of that first month back home! There was I, all keyed up and raring to go. I'd been before the Government Traffic Commissioner before I left St Dunstan's. My lorry and trailer were ready to be picked up and I had my "A" Licence, the passport which would allow me to carry goods anywhere for anybody. The local transport firms hadn't opposed my being granted one, but the Railway put in a formal protest and two weeks passed before the matter was resolved. At last, I thought. Not a bit of it! Someone had decided there must be a "handing-over" ceremony — although, thanks to St Dunstan's loan, the vehicle was bought and paid for — and that meant another two weeks' delay.

It took place in Preston at last. Lord Fraser was there, and the Mayors of Preston and Blackburn, and Dennis Foden, the Chairman of ERF, the vehicle builders, and a few other local bigwigs. This was the great moment and I was wildly excited. I could hardly wait for the speeches to be over. My two brothers were there and, as soon as the key was handed to Robert we scrambled on board.

"It looks great, Billy," Robert said, "with your name in gold, 'William Griffiths. Blackburn' on the maroon paintwork." I felt as proud as a peacock, and couldn't wait to show off my lovely new lorry and trailer to my mother and all my old friends and acquaintances. There was a secret pleasure, too, in having "W. Griffiths" back on a vehicle, just as it had been before my uncle took over the firm. When I thought about it, it all seemed hard to believe, after the despair of coming home and finding the firm on which I'd pinned my hopes gone. And now, a little over a year later, here I was with my own little business, and a brand-new lorry with W. Griffiths in gold on the door. Can you wonder I was thrilled? As we drove back to Blackburn after the ceremony, along roads which I'd cycled along a thousand times as a lad, and driven along as often in my pre-war transport days, my feelings and emotions became more and more mixed, excitement tinged with a deep disappointment that I wasn't at the wheel, happiness with an underlying sadness. But perhaps, on that day and on that journey, excitement and anticipation predominated . . . and I remember how, on the train to Glasgow, when I'd been posted overseas, I'd seen one of the family lorries with "William Griffiths (Blackburn) Ltd.", on the side, out of the window, and wondered if I should ever drive them again.

ii

The month hadn't been entirely wasted. I'd secured the promise of a contract to carry a load of large sewage pipes from Place's at Hoddlesden, near Blackburn, to Dundee, and very soon after I'd taken delivery of the vehicle — early February, 1947, I should think — I received an order for the first consignment. I would desperately have liked to see that first pay-load put on board; instead I had to be content with Robert ringing me from Dundee the following day to say that they'd delivered the load safely, the consignment note was signed, and everything was in good order. In the meantime I'd been on to a Transport Clearing House to see if they could find a return load. They could, and Robert and Alan came back from Dundee with 15 tons of jam to deliver — a thoroughly satisfactory round trip, and an auspicious start to that brand-new business: W. Griffiths, Blackburn!

I think for everyone who is seriously disabled, pride is one of the hardest things to come to terms with. One owes it to one's pride to be as independent as possible, and so one is constantly put in a position of resenting it when one's disablement leads to one receiving special treatment, and resenting it when it doesn't. In the business I had no choice but to accept whatever help came my way. An old family friend in the same line, Tom Whipp, was under contract to Place's, and would often sub-let work to me, without asking for any commission, whereas the Clearing House used to take ten per cent. If they could lay on a return load, of course, it was money well spent, and after the success of that original journey I was in high hopes. All too often, though, the vehicle would return empty, and that, of course, knocked a hole in the profits. Thanks to Tom Whipp, and to Lord Fraser, who got me a contract to carry drums of chemicals for ICI at Thornton, outward journeys were less of a problem, I usually managed to arrange maximum loads, and the vehicle was kept busy, but it was disappointing when Robert and Alan had had to hang about at their destination and nothing turned up.

The "office" of William Griffiths, Blackburn, was my room in my mother's house. There I had my typewriter and the specially adapted telephone which enabled me to run the business. I had no secretary, we couldn't run to that luxury, but I did have a young chap who came in for a couple of hours each week to do the books. I was able, through him, to keep some sort of grip on the money side, and this was vital. Not only did I have to pay the wages, I also had to find £132 a quarter to pay off the loan of £2000 from St Dunstan's. The last person to be paid was me, and many weeks there wasn't much left in the kitty!

The death of many small businesses is bad debts, and in this respect I was lucky. One builder for whom I did a minor rubble-clearing job went bust before I got paid, and I did get conned good and proper by a gent from Saffron Walden who had bought a large load of hay from one of our local farmers and wanted it delivered home. We agreed a price, I carried the hay — and that was the last I heard of him, despite numerous letters from me and my solicitors. Cleverly, he'd talked me into sending him the signed delivery note, so I had no evidence against him. I felt very bitter about it for a while — that business of pride again: had he taken advantage of my circumtances, or only of my comparative inexperience? Or a bit of both? Whichever it was, it stung me, as well as teaching me a lesson.

Generally speaking, though, the business in those early days rolled along quite smoothly. Inevitably my contribution consisted mainly of arranging jobs by telephone. I had to make sure that my contacts knew if the vehicle was available for local work, while when it was booked for a long distance run I always tried to inform the Clearing House well in advance in the hope of getting a return load. I had to keep my customers happy by ensuring that the lorry was in the right place at the right time, and soothe them when they phoned up in irate mood to complain that a load had not arrived when it should have done or not been collected on time. There was nothing unusual about situations like these, as I knew from my pre-war days. All haulage contractors experienced them, but for me there was a special satisfaction in sorting them out, for every problem solved, every detail of running the business and making a go of it, helped me to forget for a while my disabilities and the frustrations they entailed. To be involved with other people, to be part of the community, to have a job to do — that was the great thing.

And when my lorry set off for a trip to, say, London, I would often find myself picturing its progress — this was long before motorways, of course — through the centre of Blackburn, up Bull Hill, over the moors to Bolton, on to Knutsford and Stafford and on south. I could imagine Robert and Alan stopping for a cup of tea at Mrs Smith's or The Beacon or one of the other transport cafés I'd stopped at myself so often; and when, on their return, they happened to mention that they'd had a break for pie and chips at so-and-so's, it brought it all back to me with a bitter-sweet mixture of pleasure and regret.

My greatest dread was of failure. When business was quiet I would lie awake at night racked with worry about not being able to repay my loan from St Dunstan's, about letting my two brothers down, and not being able to pay their wages or meet the normal expenses of the business — let alone the unplanned ones, a new set of tyres, a breakdown, a hundred-and-one disasters, likely and unlikely! Robert, luckily, was an excellent driver, I had no worries on that score — but that was about all. Because I relied on him so heavily I tried to interest him in becoming a partner in the business, but he didn't want to know. He was quite happy to do the driving, but he had no ambitions beyond that, and no intention of taking on any responsibility for the success or failure of the business, and I came to envy him his happy-go-lucky attitude. On the bad days, and there were a few, I wondered why on earth I bothered. When you can't jot anything down or refer to a diary, when you can't simply grab the telephone and dial or even look up the number, the simplest tasks carried out without thinking by the most junior clerk become major operations. And this, remember, was just after the war, when everything was in short supply and motor fuel itself was still rationed.

Each haulier was allocated coupons for so many gallons, based on his average mileage, number of vehicles, and so on, and on one occasion I had a journey lined up and discovered to my horror that I hadn't enough coupons left to cover it: I'd overrun my allowance. In desperation I phoned the Regional Controller in Manchester and put my case — with very little expectation of getting any extra. However, he happened not only to be ex-Service and a member of the Royal British Legion, but also to know about William Griffiths, Blackburn and his one-string fiddle and let me have all I needed.

"And don't forget, Bill, if you run short again you've only to give me a ring. And good luck!"

This was one of the few occasions on which I received any special treatment. I never asked for it, but I was always delighted — and a bit ashamed — when it happened. Never mind: I had my fuel, and W. Griffiths was back on the road, and that was all that mattered.

iii

W. Griffiths might still be on the road today but for one thing, and that was the nationalization of road transport in 1947. The Transport Act, part of the great legislative programme of the post-war Labour Government which included the railways, the coal industry, and iron and steel, created the British Transport

Commission whose brief was "to create a properly integrated system of public inland transport", to include not only road haulage and the railways but the canals as well. Under the terms of the Act, the BTC was bound to acquire firms operating under "A" and "B" Licences, but only if "the undertaking . . . was carried on . . . during the whole or any part of the year 1946", and so long as it was involved "in ordinary long distance carriage for hire and reward . . ." over distances of 40 miles or more. Firms were left free to carry their own goods, but could only use private contractors for journeys of less than 25 miles.

Herbert Morrison — later Lord Morrison — says in his autobiography that "There was never any question of putting the small local haulier out of business, or of making him an employee of a nationalized industry" — and for this reason "C" licence-holders were excluded from the Bill. But, whatever the intention, it put me out of business, and for two reasons. The first was that I did not start until January 1947, and therefore did not qualify for nationalization — and therefore for compensation. The second reason was the clause about private contractors. As far as I was concerned, this meant that Tom Whipp could no longer sub-let work to me, since most of the jobs involved journeys of more than 25 miles.

Although the Transport Act passed into law in 1947 it was some time before the full effects of it hit me, and I managed to keep going through 1948 and into 1949, although things became increasingly difficult — and not only for me. A lot of small hauliers were squeezed out of business at that time. Little by little, as jobs became more difficult to get and return loads fewer and the sub-contract work dried up — even Tom Whipp could no longer help — I was forced to admit the growing possibility of failure and at the end of 1949 I finally decided to sell up. It was then that I came up against another ill effect of the nationalization. So many small firms had packed it in that lorries were two a penny, and I couldn't find a buyer for mine. I was stuck with a business that was losing money; Robert was under pressure from his uncle to go and drive for him and I had a lorry I couldn't sell and a debt that I couldn't pay off.

St Dunstan's had obviously kept an eye on my progress and, when Lord Fraser heard that I was in trouble, he got in touch with our MP at Blackburn, Barbara Castle, and the two of them did their utmost to arrange compensation for me under the Transport Act, but without success. I didn't qualify, and that was that. Eventually I did manage to sell the vehicle to W. H. Bowker, Blackburn, but at a knockdown price. Because so many lorries were available he actually did me a favour.

The failure of my transport business was a heavy blow. Despite the difficulties and anxieties, the knowledge that I was actually able to do something useful, in however limited a way, had done wonders for my morale. Just to be in touch with other people on a business footing and not simply as an object of pity, to have problems to wrestle with and the challenge of organizing runs and loads and even of coping with

109

dissatisfied or aggrieved customers, helped to take my mind off my disabilties.

They were always there, all the same; and with the business gone I was faced once more with the awful emptiness of an idle and useless life. Living at home didn't help. I was dependent, as always, on my mother and stepfather for the most basic, day-to-day functions — getting dressed and undressed, eating, washing, the toilet, things which most people do almost without thinking — and my mother, whose health wasn't good, was finding it more and more difficult to cope. She had never truly adapted to the reality of a disabled son and, although she did her best, I couldn't but feel how it weighed on her. It was as if the three years of "William Griffiths, Blackburn" had never been, and I was back to the time of my return from prison camp.

And, yet, there was a difference. Then I had only been able to picture a life without point or purpose stretching ahead like a dark tunnel with no light at the end of it, of being grudgingly looked after and being taken for little walks, a life bounded by the radio and the pitying kindness of friends and relations. Now, though on the face of it I was back to square one, I had the knowledge that I was able to do a useful job, if only I could find the right one. That was the problem.

It's difficult to describe my state of mind during the months immediately after my business came to an end, so emotionally and mentally confused did I become. Bitter disappointment alternated with a sense of achievement, a secret sense of relief that the worries of running it were over — mixed with a feeling of failure

110

and apprehension about the future. Looking back on that period now seems like remembering a disturbing dream, not quite a nightmare, but a darkening of the spirit. As before, I turned to the radio to help pass the time and take my mind off my troubles: plays, serials especially, as they left one with something to look forward to, comedy programmes, anything and everything. I must have been the BBC's best customer! And when the radio failed me, I would rig up my trombone and have a good old blow on that!

Perhaps the worst part was the feeling of being housebound. I had never imagined that I should look back to the years in prison camp with anything but relief that they were over, but there, at least, with my stick grasped in that Heath Robinson contraption of tin cans and wire, I'd been able to wander off through the camp unescorted, and that had made all the difference. But now, in this world of freedom, I couldn't even do that. The crab claw artificial hands were not adapted to hold a stick, and even if they had been, the thought of trying to navigate the streets was far worse than having to run the gauntlet of the Japanese guards. So, unless someone offered to take me out, I was stuck at home.

Luckily I'd made the acquaintance of an ex-service chap by the name of Sid Wilding. Sid was unmarried, and I daresay he was lonely, or perhaps he was simply sorry for me. At any rate, Sid used to come round two or three nights a week and we would go out together, sometimes to the pub, sometimes to one or other of a couple of working-men's clubs where there would be a show of some kind, sometimes a comedian, at others

111

a concert. I became a member, and was able to feel like a part of the human race again. Sid was a bit of a comedian himself, a lively, outgoing type who had served along with Frankie Howerd in his ENSA days and knew him well, and he often took part in the club shows, singing a song or telling a few jokes. Sid, with his jokes and his cheerfulness and his kindness in taking me round with him, was a tonic for me. He was also indirectly responsible for completely changing my life.

iv

This was how it started. We'd gone to the club one night as usual, and Sid had left me to talk to some pals, so I was sitting by myself when I heard a woman's voice say, "Billy, this is Ivy Walkden. You won't remember me, but you might remember my niece, Alice Jolly?"

"Of course," I said, "I remember Alice very well. She tried to teach me to dance in the old days."

"That's right." She laughed. "She must have forgiven you for stepping on her toes because she says she'd like to see you again. I was talking to her only yesterday."

"Great," I said. "I'd love to meet her again."

"I'll tell her, and we'll arrange something."

She left me then, and my mind went back to those days before the war, when a whole crowd of us used to go about together. Ethel, my ex-wife, had been one, and Alice had been another. There'd never been anything between us, just the jokey, lighthearted kind of pallyness you get when a bunch of youngsters go off to the cinema or dances together, a lot of laughter and teasing and daftness and holding hands at the back of the ninepennies and a quick kiss when you saw a girl home — if you were lucky. That was how it used to be then, at any rate, and although I'd got off with Ethel, Alice was around, one of the gang, a good sort, I remembered, full of life and fun. Yes, it would be nice to meet again — but what would she think when she saw *me*? Obviously she'd know what to expect — but that wasn't the same thing as being faced with the reality. I didn't know what I looked like, though I did know, because I'd been told, that even after all this time my face was still pitted with the marks of the powder-burns from the explosion, and I imagined that I was not a pretty sight. Still, she'd said she'd like us to meet again, and that was good enough for me.

Ivy Walkden — soon to become Auntie Ivy — was as good as her word, and the following week I was picked up and taken to tea at Alice's. I don't remember if there was any awkwardness at first. It seems that very soon we were chatting about the old days and people we'd both known, and there was a lot of laughter and codding, and I said to Alice, "Why didn't you get in touch before?"

"Oh," she said, "I didn't think you'd remember me and, anyway, I thought you were involved with your own friends."

"What are you doing now?" I asked her.

"Still singing," she said. "Not with a dance band, though — mostly with club concerts."

"You've not been to ours, then?"

"Oh yes I have," she said, laughing, "but you weren't there."

"We'll have to see about you coming again."

It was a good reunion, and it set the mood for all that was to happen afterwards. I felt a warmth and friendliness towards me that I'd hardly known during all those years, not the compassionate warmth of pity but the other kind that normal people feel towards each other, liking, affection, on equal terms. I went home knowing how much I'd missed that, and how badly I needed it; afraid, too, that, like my business, it might be a mirage, for where could it lead? Alice was married and had a young son; she had her own life, and I knew it had been a hard one. Her father had been gassed on the Somme in the First War, and had become a proud and bitter man, too proud to apply for his war disability pension, so that the family had always been short of money, and Alice herself had had to go out to work for a time in one of the local textile mills at fourteen. Later she trained as a nanny and worked for the Causey family in Blackburn. George Causey was the Borough Engineer, and Alice had been happy with them; in fact she is still friendly with them, and the two little girls she looked after are both married. Then, during the war, she'd worked on a valve assembly line at Mullard's, and singing with a dance band in the evenings to help make ends meet. The background had had its influence on her and me, for the Griffiths, with their own road haulage business, were felt to be a cut above her family. We had our own house, which my grandfather had built, up on Whalley Old Road, while they lived in a

114

terrace house down in the town; and Alice confessed to me once later that when we were both youngsters she'd felt she "wasn't good enough for me": bloody daft, but that's how it was in the closely-knit working class society in a Lancashire mill town before the war.

That, like many other things, had changed; if anything, the tables had been turned, and depressed and nervous as I was at that time, I felt I wasn't good enough for her. But Alice said when I was leaving, "Why not come to one of my concerts, you and Sid?" and I muttered something to the effect that I'd like to, and we left it at that. The more I thought about it, though, the better idea it seemed, and I set about finding where she was booked to sing, and Sid and I went along, and afterwards the three of us would sit and have a drink together.

From there it was only a matter of time before Auntie Ivy and her husband Harold invited Sid and me to go along with them and Alice to her concerts, and this became a regular thing. She often used to appear with a smashing local comedian by the name of Ron Ward, and these evenings became the high point of my life. There was music and laughter and fun and a sense of true friendship and, increasingly, the feeling that Alice was taking me under her wing in the nicest, most disinterested way — which wasn't entirely disinterested! Secretly, I believe, even then she was scouting round for something for me to do, for she had quickly realized the vacuum that the end of my business had left in my life, and the state of nervous depression which this, in conjunction with living at home, had reduced me to.

"We *must* find something for him to do", she said to Aunt Ivy, and in her energetic, practical way she set about doing so.

I knew nothing of this at the time. I merely continued to go with the others to her concerts whenever possible. Quite often at these affairs I would be left alone at the table and occasionally found myself the target of well-meaning bores who would start to cross-question me about my injuries. This was a subject I did not wish to be reminded about, and one time when a total stranger asked me how I'd lost my hands, I said to him, "Well, it was like this, you see. I was eating a dish of pig's trotters and chips, and they were so delicious, before I knew what was happening I'd eaten half my arm away as well."

Not the height of repartee, perhaps, but it settled him. He shot off and I heard no more from him. It's an odd thing, incidentally, how certain people feel they're at liberty to ask one the most personal questions, simply because one has some obvious disablement, just as others will behave as if one's deaf as well as blind and talk about one in the third person although one's standing next to them. "Do you think Billy would care to do so-and-so or such-and-such?" they'll say, and you begin to feel like the Invisible Man. That was mostly with strangers. On several other occasions, because my artificial eyes were so lifelike, those who didn't know me found it hard to believe I couldn't see as well as they could. "About time that bugger got a job," my mother heard one woman say to another on the bus, and even my doctor, the first time I went to see him, asked me, "Do you have any sight at all?" Perhaps the best story of all, though, was one time when I'd had to go to Manchester Eye Hospital for a check-up on my eye sockets, and I was being led out through the waiting-room, and I heard one woman say to another, "Ee, Maggie, I think we'd better go; they don't seem to have done *him* much good!"

I suppose you can survive most of life's setbacks and disasters so long as you don't lose your sense of humour. Sometimes, I must admit, I was in danger of losing mine, but then something comical or droll would happen, or be said, to restore one's sense of proportion. If you can laugh there's hope for you.

That's by the way. There were really two bright spots during this rather dreary period. One was the concerts, and through them, gradually getting to know Alice better. The other was my visits to Ian Fraser House. I could go there whenever I felt the need for a break, or to give my mother one, and it was always with pleasure and a sense of relief. Although I was growing more accustomed to being without sight or hands, it was good to be among friends and in a place where to be blind was normal. At this time, too, at the beginning of the '50s, there was a move to introduce sport for the disabled. As far as the blind were concerned, this matched Sir Arthur Pearson's theory that the more active and normal their lives could be made, the happier they would be. I can vouch for the truth of this, and by coincidence it fitted in with my increasing reliance on Alice.

CHAPTER
FOUR

A Fresh Start

i

"If *you* don't take him," Aunt Ivy said to Alice one day in 1952, "then *I* will!"

I didn't hear the conversation of which this was a part, but I was told about it afterwards. What had happened was this. My mother's health was getting worse, and it was becoming obvious to those friends and relations who saw her regularly that she could no longer cope with looking after me. There was a great deal of discussion as to what was to be done, and finally the local St Dunstan's Welfare Officer, who knew the situation, went to see mother and Alice and suggested that Alice should take me in as a paying guest. Mother was relieved to be free of the burden, and Alice, bless her, was willing to take it on, even though it meant giving up her job. And so it came about that I moved out of mother's house, and into my own room in Alice's, just across the Park, and into a life which, in the course of a few years, was to be utterly transformed.

Alice's marriage had, by this time, fallen apart, and she and her husband were legally separated. Her son

Bobby was eleven and living with her, and she was afraid that if she were to sue for a divorce at that time it might have unfortunate effects on him. He was a lovely lad, lively and full of fun like his mother, and he and I got on like a house on fire. My lack of sight and hands didn't seem to bother him at all and we built up a relationship between us more like a couple of brothers than a man of thirty-two and a young boy. That was another bonus from the arrangement, one of many.

Before this, at one of Alice's concert engagements, she'd said to me, "You know, Billy, I've heard how you used to sing when you were in POW camp. Why don't you come along to my singing teacher and take some lessons?"

I had to laugh. "That was nothing," I said. "I just used to warble away to myself when I was wandering round to cheer myself up. I can't sing."

"How do you know you can't?"

"And even if I could," I said, "can you imagine me standing up in public, singing? It'd empty the house!"

She didn't say any more then, but later on she mentioned it again. By this time I'd thought a bit more about it, and it didn't seem quite such a daft idea as it had at first. I'd always enjoyed music and was happy to join in when there was a sing-song; it would be something else to occupy my mind — and anyway, what was there to lose? So I said,

"All right, I'll have a go. But don't blame me if Harry lets out a yell and covers his ears."

I knew Harry Dinsdale and his family, nice people who wouldn't be too hard on me; so eventually Alice took me along. Harry sat himself down at the piano, and I stood there feeling a right mug. "I'll play a scale," he said, "and I want you to sing it — just to get an idea of your voice." This went on for a bit, and I did the best I could. He stopped playing and said, "That's not too bad. I'm going to give you a piece of music to learn. When you've mastered it, come back and we'll see."

The "piece of music", called "Hear the Song and the Singer", turned out to consist of ten pages, music and words. "I'll never learn all that lot," I said. "Yes you will," said Alice. I was beginning to learn that when Alice Jolly had decided that something was to happen, happen it did, and over the next two weeks she went over that blooming song with me it must have been a hundred times, until I had it fixed in my head. I didn't have a tape-recorder then, and it must have driven her up the wall because I'm a slow learner at the best of times. It was like being back at school again, and one thing I came to realize was how hard she had to work in preparing for her concerts. Anyway, we persevered and at last I felt ready to go back to Harry's and give it a go.

"Splendid!" Harry said, when I'd been through it without stumbling or forgetting the words. "That wasn't too bad at all." He then told me very gently where I'd gone wrong and made suggestions as to how I could improve. The real surprise, though, was that I'd found I quite enjoyed it. The mental effort of learning the song, and the concentration needed to perform it, even in front of an audience of three in Harry and Renee's lounge, were exactly the sort of stimulus I lacked. Listening to the radio was all very well, but it was passive: singing, like running the business, was active and, when I was involved with it, everything else was forgotten. Don't imagine from this that I thought of myself as the new Caruso! I knew I had a pleasant baritone voice and could sing in tune and that was all. But that was all that mattered. I couldn't have cared less whether it would ever lead anywhere. In fact, it never occurred to me that it might — least of all to the Festival Hall, the Old Vic or television.

Alice and I went away after that first "recital" with another piece for me to learn, and each time we went back and I did my piece Harry encouraged me to continue, until, one day, he said,

"You're coming on well, Billy. It's time you went and had some proper lessons."

"Are you serious?" I said. Then Alice chimed in, "I agree with you, Harry."

Harry went on, "I've spoken to Tom Bridge, and he's prepared to teach you. How about it?"

"Well," I said, "I don't know. Do you think I'm good enough?"

"Yes, I do, but you need proper professional training, and I think Tom's your man."

Tom Bridge was well known locally as a singer and teacher of music and the upshot was that I signed on with him for a course of lessons. Each one lasted half-an-hour and was mainly concerned with voice production. I got on well with Tom and his wife, Clarice, and the more I studied the subject and the more I learnt about expression and how to project your voice, the more absorbed in it I became, and I realized that what I had felt right at the beginning was true: singing, even at this humble level, supplied one of the main things that my life lacked. It was something — admittedly with help, but then I should always need help with most things — something that I could *do*. There were a million things I couldn't do, but you don't need eyes or hands to sing.

The other main lack in my life was also being taken care of. From the time when Alice and I first met again, through Auntie Ivy, we had found we enjoyed each other's company. A true friendship quickly developed until, one day, we discovered we were in love with each other. I can truly say that from that moment life took on a meaning and a purpose and a happiness which I had never imagined possible in my wildest dreams.

ii

As time went by I became more and more absorbed in this business of singing — I even gave up smoking! — and Alice encouraged me to consider the possibility of, one day, singing in public. I resisted. The very thought of such a thing made me go cold inside, but, rather as the idea of starting the transport business seemed to gather momentum until I realized there was no stopping it, so did music. After some months of having lessons with Tom Bridge, Alice said to me one day,

"I'm going to ask Mrs Fee if she thinks her husband will take you on."

"Steady on, Alice," I said, "I'm not in their class and never will be."

"Never mind that. I'll just ask her."

Harry Fee and his wife were first-class pianists and specialized in training and preparing singers for the music festivals and competitions which took place in various towns round Blackburn. We knew them slightly, but I didn't imagine they'd even consider trying to teach me. In fact, I felt it was a bit of cheek even to ask them. However, as I said before, when Alice gets an idea in her head she's not easily discouraged and a few days later she said,

"Mrs Fee's just rung, and she says, bring Billy round, with a copy of some song he knows, and Harry will hear him."

Well! We've often had a good laugh since about that first audition with Harry Fee. He was a perfectionist and I was very far from perfect. In fact, I was so nervous I made a complete hash of the song. "You should've seen his face!" Alice said afterwards. "The poor man was in agony!" It can't have been quite as bad as all that, because he agreed to help me, or it may simply have been that he knew I was already having lessons with Tom Bridge, or that he was sorry for me. At least he realized that I was prepared to work at it, which I was. St Dunstan's had helped me buy a tape recorder, one I was able to operate by myself, and this made all the difference. No longer did Alice have to spend hours going through the words and music over and over again until I got them into my thick head. I could shut myself up in my room and learn them, and practise them, alone, and this I did. I suppose I'm quite a determined person — Alice would say stubborn! —

123

and now I had something to be determined about. Moreover, my two teachers didn't stand for any nonsense. Everything, the way you stood, the way you held your head, tone, phrasing, had to be right. And, little by little, I began to gain confidence, though I still couldn't imagine myself standing up in front of an audience — an audience I couldn't see — not able to have a copy of the music, not even able to mop my perspiring brow. And I never would have done if it hadn't been for my ever-patient teachers who were prepared to spend time and take the trouble to coach me, and Alice to goad and encourage me. I was on a roller-coaster and there was no jumping off.

Eventually, after many months of lessons, Harry Fee said to me one day,

"There's a music festival at Burnley coming up in three months' time, and it includes a competition for solo male voices. I think you should enter."

I shall never forget those three months. By the end of them I was a nervous wreck. Talk about stage-fright! I practised and practised until I was repeating the words of the chosen song in my sleep, but how was I to know what would happen when I stood up there in front of the judges in Burnley Town Hall? Would I "dry" halfway through? Well, if I did, I was damn sure it wouldn't be for want of effort on my part.

At last the dreaded evening arrived. Alice heard me through a "final" final rehearsal, made sure my tie was straight and my "dress hands" weren't going to fall off, and away we went. There were ten of us in the competition. I was no. 5. To be honest, I can't remember that much about the evening. All I do know is that when my turn came, Alice led me on to the platform and made sure I was pointing in the right direction. The pianist played the introductory notes, I sang my song without any dreadful mistakes, and Alice came and rescued me and I sat down and waited for the verdict.

A voice said, "Number five?"

Up went my arm. There was a pause, and then the adjudicator said, "Well, my man, you stand remarkably well —" and that was all. Not a word about my voice or my rendering of the song. I'd been rigidly at attention, afraid of not doing it properly, and petrified of falling off the stage! The song, I shall never forget, was "Trade Winds", words by John Masefield, music by Frederick Keel; and relief that it was over just about outweighed my disappointment at not being offered — publicly, at any rate — a word of criticism or encouragement about my singing. However, at the end of the competition, I was given the judges' report, and if it wasn't exactly flattering at least it gave me something to work on.

"Never mind, Billy," Alice said, "you did all right." And if she wasn't, perhaps, being completely impartial, what did it matter? After all the months of lessons, the hours of rehearsing, the sheer terror, I had actually stood up there, in public, and sung; and if all that the judges could find to say was that, not to worry. I'd do better next time.

iii

That's enough about singing for the moment. It was only part of the new direction my life was taking, now that Alice and I were together. That relationship was the centre, to which everything else was related and from which everything else stemmed. One thing that stemmed from it, if only indirectly, was sport. I was still going back to Ian Fraser House from time to time, partly to give Alice a break, partly because to be with other blind and disabled people is a source of strength and comfort. I used to find this at home with Alice's cousin's little girl, Pat, who was spastic and completely helpless. She died when she was only sixteen, but, while she was alive, I used to visit her quite often, and always made sure I had some little treat in my jacket pocket for her. I couldn't see her smile, but I could hear her little shriek of delight when I arrived, and feel her desperate efforts — her hands were useless — to reach it. When, after a minute or two, it was given to her there would be more gurgles of pleasure; then the little helpless girl and I would sit together for a while, and I am sure that we shared, because of our mutual, though very different, disabilities, some communion of the spirit which was above and beyond ordinary earthly happiness. I know I felt it, and I think she did too.

This sense of the blind, the crippled, the disabled, all being, as it were, in the same boat was very strong at St Dunstan's. It had nothing to do with self-pity, but was based on the knowledge that, however severe one's own handicap, one wasn't alone; indeed, there were others

126

far worse off. This came home to me on one occasion when I was out walking, following the railings in the grounds of Ian Fraser House, and I bumped into someone else doing the same circuit. We greeted each other and I realized he was a young man who I knew only slightly, who had been blinded as a result of a head wound during the Korean War. As we walked along together, he warned me that he might lose his sense of direction since his wound sometimes proved "a bit of a nuisance" and played tricks on him. Sure enough, quite soon he had to stop and wait for his head to clear. Yet he accepted this "nuisance" quite philosophically and seemed more concerned about me getting lost or coming a cropper than he was about himself. There was something in his calm acceptance of his own misfortunes — totally blind, and subject to blackouts — which made me feel strangely sad, yet glad to be with him. Perhaps courage, like 'flu, is catching.

Being able to walk freely in the grounds was one of the joys of staying at Ovingdean, for it was not something I had been able to do at home, and I was always worried about keeping fit. It was at about this period that the provision of sports for the disabled first got under way for me and this was to have almost as profound an effect on my life as music. St Dunstan's, following Sir Arthur Pearson's conviction that the more normal a blind person's life can be made the better, encouraged members to take part in as many different sports as possible and their research department came up with all sorts of ingenious gadgets that enabled us, unlikely as it sounds, to shoot with bow and rifle, to bowl, to fish and to put the shot. There was an annual Sports Meeting at Ian Fraser House, and the first time I entered, for as many events as possible, my results were so abysmal that I determined to settle down to some serious training.

Swimming, at which I had been quite respectable as a youngster, was one thing I reckoned I could do, both as a sport in itself and as a way of keeping fit. Thanks to the manager of the baths in Blackburn, who allowed me to practise after hours, and to Tom Dewhurst, the instructor there, I put in many hours. Breaststroke, front and back crawl. Tom coached me in all of them. In between, I would go with Alice or Bobby simply to have a swim. I loved it. I suppose everyone shuts their eyes when they dive, but there is a difference between looking first, judging height and distance and then diving, and springing off the edge literally "blind."

I soon became quite used to doing that, but, on one occasion I'm not likely to forget, I was swimming happily about in the pool when I got cramp. Immediately I made for where I reckoned the edge of the pool was, and realized with a sudden panic that even if I reached it I shouldn't be able to grab the rail. Fortunately for me Bobby was in the water, keeping an eye on me, and piloted me to the side. Otherwise this story might have ended at the deep end of Blackburn Public Swimming Baths!

But I also needed practice and training for field and track events. For simple exercise there was the park opposite where Alice lived. At first I would only go for a walk there if someone was with me, but then young Bobby, who often accompanied me, said to me one day,

"You know, Billy, there's a low wall all around the park. I reckon if you could keep close to it, just brushing it with the edge of your outside foot, you could come here for walks on your own. Try it."

So I did. I had a few stumbles at first, but once I'd got the idea I found it quite easy, and it became a regular outing. It was good for my sense of balance. Above all, it was something else I could do by myself. Every scrap of independent action I could achieve was precious to me, and instinctively Bobby understood this, just as Alice does. Help, over so many things, one unfortunately has to have; pampering one does not; and to be robbed of doing things, however trivial, which one can do for oneself is bad for one's self-respect. Some spouses of blind people cannot grasp this and treat their blind partners as if they were made of glass. Treat a man as if he's afflicted, Sir Arthur Pearson said, and he'll become afflicted. To which I could add, encourage a blind person to be as capable and independent as possible and he will, within the limits of his affliction, achieve ability and independence. And, of course, if you happen to be short of hands as well as eyes it's even more important.

My circuits of the park, monitored from a distance by jolly Auntie Beatty, another of Alice's aunts, were not always unnoticed or uneventful. On one occasion some little boys were, as far as I could gather, trying to lift a hefty fallen bough over the wall, fuel for their Guy Fawkes bonfire. They called to me.

"Hey, mister, give us a hand."

That was one thing I couldn't give them, and I said, "Sorry, I can't. I'm — er — too busy."

As I walked on, keeping close to my guiding wall as usual, I heard one of them say disgustedly, "Tchah, skinny bugger!" Instead of resenting this remark, as you might have expected, it rather pleased me. It meant that they hadn't noticed my cautious navigation round the perimeter, nor the fact that I wasn't in any state to help them, much as I would like to have done — a curious twist of pride I suppose, a sign of that constant, wistful longing to be regarded as normal.

Another time someone stopped me and asked, in a rather peremptory tone of voice, "Where are you going?"

"I'm just having a stroll round the park," I said. "Why?"

"Where do you live?"

Although I felt like telling him to mind his own business, I replied politely enough.

"Just down the road, since you ask."

There was a silence, and I thought this queer and rather impertinent interrogation was over. Not a bit of it. The next question was,

"Why are you wearing leather gloves on such a warm afternoon?" Obviously he, whoever he was, hadn't realized that I was wearing my dress hands. Suddenly I had an idea.

"Are you a policeman?" I asked.

That really did it. "Are you trying to be funny?" he demanded in an unpleasant voice. "What d'you think this uniform is?"

"I'm sorry," I said, "but I happen to be blind. These eyes you see are artificial, and so are the hands inside the gloves. That's why I wear them."

Poor bloke! I'm sure he didn't know where to look. "I do beg your pardon, sir. I'd no idea. You see, I'm new to the area, and we've had a run of burglaries, so I'm on the look-out for anything suspicious, and the gloves . . ."

His voice trailed off, and I said,

"Don't worry about it, you're not the first person to be fooled. Even my doctor, the first time I went to see him, asked me if I had any sight at all."

I guessed he was a young copper, so I didn't embarrass him further by suggesting that burglars only put gloves on when they're actually on the job! Or so I imagine.

That wasn't the only time I have, quite unintentionally, caused the police embarrassment. Alice and I were on our way home from a long stay in Brighton, and our Morris Minor was packed to the roof. It was so full, in fact, that we'd had to tie the boot lid shut with string. Anyway, we were bowling along the M1 when a police car came roaring past with lights on and siren blaring, overtook us and flagged us down. Alice was really worried.

"I wasn't even doing seventy," she said to me as she pulled in to the hard shoulder. "Whatever's wrong?"

Two policemen came over to us and one of them said to Alice,

"Good afternoon, madam. I just want to look in the back of your car."

"Go ahead," said Alice, and got out. There, hanging down by its harness, was one of my spare artificial hands which had slipped out from under the lid. Someone had noticed it and rung up the police to say they'd seen a car pass and it had a body in the back!

Another time we were crawling through Blackburn in heavy traffic. I was sitting in the back, smoking a cigarette which I realized I would have to get rid of pretty quick as it was beginning to burn my lips. I couldn't take it out, and Alice couldn't stop to take it out for me. The only thing I could do was wind the window down with my elbow and spit it out into the road. I wasn't to know that at that precise moment we were passing a copper on point duty, and that I'd scored a bullseye on his tunic!

"Billy!" Alice said in her most reproachful voice, and managed to stop and went back to apologize. Luckily he was one who knew us and we had a good laugh about it. But I wasn't allowed to forget it, and later, though not for that reason, I gave up smoking, no doubt to the relief of Blackburn's traffic police.

I know I go on a bit about the longing to be "normal" — or at least to be treated as such — and I think it's something all disabled people feel. It was especially strong for me in the early days, and this was where Bobby was so good for my morale. He did accept me as normal, would jump on my back and start mock fights with me, would come swimming with me, make me stay with him when he mowed the lawn, and drag me back if I slunk off, would tease me and treat me exactly as if I were a pal or a brother. At the same time, he had no qualms about taking out my eyes, washing them and putting them back — which he would do quick as a flash — or helping me put on the crab's claws or my dress hands. I'm sure that sometimes he pretended to himself to be blind and handless in order to get some idea of my difficulties and find ways of helping me. It is a rare gift, and one which he puts to good and compassionate purpose now, when he runs a home for the elderly.

Others found it more difficult to regard me as a sentient being, never mind normal, in all but a few insignificant ways. I've heard people say to Alice, as if I was deaf as well as blind, "Do you think *he* would like to do so-and-so?" when they were standing next to me; or, well within my hearing, "He does look old!" or "I shouldn't think he'll live long", or "What a job, looking after *him*!" Or, on one occasion, when I was enjoying an evening out with my cousins and they'd become involved with some acquaintances at the next table, I heard a young man saying to one of our group, "What do you say if we run your blind pal home and go off and have a meal somewhere?" If I'd had even one hand and could open a door, I'd have left. If I'd had one hand and one eye and been able to see the ignorant little twerp I'd have punched him on the nose! No one likes to be written off like that.

But I was talking about sport, not about being sorry for myself. I needed more than toddling round the park if I was to do any good in the disabled games. I needed to practise race-walking and sprinting. There was a playing field within reach of where we lived and Alice and I used to go there regularly for my training sessions. She would pace out a hundred yards, set me pointing in the right direction, and then take up a position somewhere beyond the finishing line. "On your marks! Ready. Go!" and off I set in what I hoped was the right direction as fast as I could. It's not easy to keep straight if you can't see, and Alice would yell "Left, left, left" or "Right, right, right" as I wandered off course. When I kept on line, she would give me "Good, good, good," usually followed by a shout of "Left!" or "Right!", and finally, as I crossed the finishing line, "Stop!" She timed each sprint, and this gave me a goal to aim for.

For race-walking we adapted the old system by which a blindfolded donkey was employed to go round and round a central pivot grinding corn or hauling water or whatever. I was the donkey, with a rope round my waist and the other end looped over a stake in the ground. The rope was about ten yards long, and by keeping it taut I could circle the post without any assistance, though Alice timed each circuit, kept a count, and kept a critical eye on my heel-and-toe action. Each time, I tried to improve on my previous performance, and when I succeeded, the sense of achievement was almost as satisfactory as actually taking part in proper races. These training sessions

134

usually ended up with the long jump. I would stand on the start line, grit my teeth and take an almighty spring straight ahead and slightly upwards, trying to imagine I was flying, and land with a thump, trying not to fall backwards.

From 1950 until a few years ago I regularly took part in St Dunstan's Annual Sports, and thoroughly enjoyed it. All the training in the world would never have brought me to Olympic standards, or even to a state in which I was ever likely to win prizes competing with other disabled people, but winning wasn't the object of the exercise. The pleasure lay in the taking part, in trying to do better than in the previous year, and in the fellowship with the other participants. We were all in the business of trying to forget our disabilities by overcoming them as much as possible, and getting as much fun and excitement out of life as we could. We all knew that we were no great champions, but that wasn't the point. We were stretching ourselves to the limits of our ability and that, important for everyone, is especially important for the disabled whose opportunities are so much fewer and harder to come by.

I think to many ordinary people the idea of the disabled taking part in sport seems fairly amazing, but of course it isn't at all. In fact, because our sports are truly amateur, you could say that it is sport as it should be, performed for the sense of prowess and the enormous pleasure it gives. The disabled don't take part to make money, and I very much doubt if any of us are using anabolic stearoids! People are justly surprised, though, when they learn that someone without hands

135

can put the shot. That this is possible is due to Norman French, of St Dunstan's Research and Inventions Department. He came up with a device consisting essentially of a long, stout leather gauntlet with a cup at the end in which the shot rests. The gauntlet was attached firmly to my right forearm, which I then had to hold vertically upwards until I brought back my arm and launched the shot. It was quite tricky and I didn't break the world record, but at least it was another skill learnt — and sometimes good for a laugh. Norman even produced a simple method of launching a sling ball. A narrow leather strap was attached to the ball, and I tucked the end of it into the crook of my elbow. By swinging my arm backwards and forwards with increasing momentum I was able to send it a fair distance. The fact that I never won any major prizes didn't bother me one bit; I never expected to. I had other, and better, reasons for taking part than pot-hunting. Imagine my surprise and delight, therefore, when, in 1969 — this is running ahead of my story — I was awarded the trophy for Disabled Sportsman of the Year by the Sportswriters Association of Great Britain — recommended, I learnt later, by Sir Ludwig Guttman of Stoke Mandeville fame. It made all the "donkey-work" seem doubly worthwhile.

iv

After that first nerve-racking singing competition I took my courage in both, well, stumps, and entered regularly, and gradually became more confident. I still went through the same anxiety for the fortnight or so beforehand as I struggled to become word-perfect; but the ordeal of actually standing up there on my own and singing became less agonizing as time went on. I rarely won; but a decent mark and some helpful criticism were all I needed in the way of encouragement. Quite often I came second or third, and I remember one occasion in particular when I did win — to my amazement, for I was worn out with nerves. I'd had to sing twice, once in the morning, then again in the evening, and each time the adjudicator had made me repeat the performance because he couldn't make up his mind. Finally I tied with one of the other competitors, and we were made to go through a "sing-off". I hated these. I'd have put everything into the first rendering and felt I had nothing left. But this time I must have had some reserve for I won by half a mark. But again, though winning was nice, it was the least of the reasons I did it for.

At more and more of the places where Alice used to sing professionally — clubs and so on — they were introducing microphones, which she hated. Amplification alters both the technique and the atmosphere of concert work, and she finally gave it up altogether and concentrated on singing for various charities. All the time we were observing each other's progress, and one day she suggested that we practise a duet together with the idea of performing at a forthcoming charity concert. This was the beginning of a "partnership in song" which has continued right up to this day and has given both of us enormous pleasure and satisfaction. At the same time we both continued to sing solo, and eventually, in the early 'sixties, I was awarded the Oscar Clifton Trophy at the Southport Music Festival, which did a lot for my confidence and, if anything, increased my enthusiasm.

From the time that Alice and I realized that we loved each other it was inevitable that, when circumstances allowed, we should get married. In fact, although she got divorced in 1959, it wasn't until three years later that I finally "popped the question".

"Yes," she replied, "— with Bobby's permission."

So I went and asked Bobby's permission, and he said, "What took you so long?", which cleared that up satisfactorily, though I would have been hard put to it to answer his question. Was it that my new-found happiness with her seemed to me such a precious thing, and so complete as it was, that I was afraid to disturb it? Was it that deep down I still lacked the self-confidence to believe that anyone could really be prepared to put up with me for life? I don't know, and it doesn't matter. All that matters is that she accepted me with Bobby's enthusiastic permission and we were duly married at Audley Range United Reform Church on 26 May, 1962 and have never regretted it. And that's over twenty-five years ago!

A few other people must have been asking each other Bobby's question. My mother was delighted, so were Alice's family, all of whom by this time I knew well and liked tremendously. Her father, as I have already mentioned, was a sad figure, his life ruined by his experiences in the First War; but her mother was great fun with a lively sense of humour, and Denis and Edward, her two brothers-in-law, were both ex-Service; one had served in Burma. We were always welcome in their homes. For a long time I had been treated as if I were a member of the family. Now I was, and it was a good feeling.

Not long after we were married Bobby seemed unusually quiet and thoughtful, and I asked him if anything was troubling him.

"Not troubling," he said, and paused. "I've been thinking. Now you two are really both my parents, I'd like to change my name to Griffiths. Would you agree?"

Nothing could have pleased me better. As I hope I've made clear, we had a splendid relationship, fond and easy, and anything that bound the three of us more closely together could only increase my sense of security and happiness. So he went off to see a solicitor and, after a deal of trouble, for all his examination credentials and things had to be altered, he changed his name by deed poll.

For me it was all like a miracle. The no-hoper who had returned from POW camp seventeen years before, who had been through a fair number of bouts of desolation and despair, suddenly found himself with a load of interests, and surrounded by a loving family. If I'd had any fingers, I'd have pinched myself to make sure I wasn't dreaming it all.

CHAPTER
FIVE

This is Your Life

i

In November, 1969, after Bill had been voted
Disabled Sportsman of the Year and awarded
their trophy, Sir Edward Dunlop wrote to Profes-
sor Sir Ludwig Guttmann, Head of Stoke
Mandeville Hospital, from Melbourne, to say
how greatly the news had "uplifted" him. Recalling that awesome moment when he had had to
decide whether it would be a kindness to try and
save Bill's life or not, he went on:

"I maintained my belief in man's unquenchable
spirit and intelligence which could open other
doors even if he seemed imprisoned by darkness
and helplessness. Further I promised a Court of
Enquiry if anything happened to Bill within my
hospital! . . . His subsequent career, with his successful entry into a transport business, and the
remarkable way that he has triumphed over such
formidable disabilities, you must know, for the
man is a legend . . . So I am utterly thrilled that

the flickering candle of life I cared for in
Bandoeng has come to burn so much brighter
than I could have imagined. He is very much
your protégé and admirer so I congratulate you
too."

"The man is a legend . . ." That was written
nearly twenty years ago; much has happened
since to support it. The previous twenty-four
years can be seen as a prolonged and often har-
rowing period of adjustment to the limitations of
being blind and without hands, of gradually
returning self-confidence, of discovering fresh
possibilities in life, even when so desperately
handicapped. During the years after that Bill was
to build on those foundations.

Five factors in particular were responsible for
the transformation, all of them interlocked, and
first and foremost is Bill's own staunchly
independent character. That, with its inherent
qualities of courage, humour and perseverance,
was evident in POW camp from the moment he
was able to hobble about again, and has never
failed through all the setbacks and disappoint-
ments since. Second one must put his meeting
with Alice again, and her practical and
unsentimental devotion to him over nearly thirty
years. In character they complement each other
admirably: her brusqueness against his stubborn-
ness, her determination and humour against his,
and their shared love of music, the third factor. It

141

was she who pushed him into singing; while St Dunstan's, the fourth, which first started the process of rehabilitation, and whose importance ever since cannot be overstated, introduced him to sport, the fifth element.

"Bill", St Dunstan's Sports Officer, Jock Carnochan, wrote of him in 1970, "is finding there are lots of things he can do that he never thought possible. He has the determination to do it. He has the interest to do it." And Norman French, who designed many of the gadgets which enabled Bill to throw the javelin, put the shot, take part in rifle-shooting and ten-pin bowling, said of him, "He has always been among the foremost in using adaptations for the handless man, he has always had a go. Whether it has been a failure or not he is always willing to try." And he quotes Bill's remark after his first pretty dismal entry into St Dunstan's sports, "My, they're all professionals here. If I'd known I'd have brought my pumps with me." And, as Bill himself says in his self-deprecating way, "I'm not anything brilliant or wonderful. I just take part for the fun and do the best I can." In that one sentence lies the secret.

It has been necessary to interrupt Bill's own story at this point because these are matters in which he is unlikely to do himself justice. At the same time one has to remember that they are the high points of a life which is never remotely easy by normal standards. Apart from typewriter, telephone, tape recorder, radio — and the lavatory, which we shall eventually and inevitably come to — almost all the routine actions of daily life are impossible to him. You try getting up in the morning as he has to.

ii

When I wake up I invariably creep into my combined office and study, with its various gadgets, but first I have to put on a dressing-gown. I grasp it between my stumps, fumble for the sleeves and, having found them, push my short arms into them. It's always a tussle to tie the cord round my waist, but putting on slippers is easy. So long as "no one" has moved them, I can just slide my feet into them. At home, of course, I know my way about "blindfold", though I always keep my arms, my "bumpers", held out in front of my body in case I do happen to walk into something. They don't hurt, my nose does.

Once safely in my office, I can either switch on my old friend, the radio, or the latest edition of the "talking newspaper." I get one from Blackburn and the other from Blackpool. They're produced by volunteers in the two towns from items in the local press and keep one up to date on what's going on. For the wider world there's the News on Radio 4, and I usually catch their bulletins during my early morning session.

Often I have a song to learn for a forthcoming concert, and this is an opportunity to work on it. I get it on tape as soon as possible, then, during my pre-breakfast sessions, I play it over and over to memorize words and music, singing softly to myself while I do so. When St Dunstans' appointed me to be their Public Relations representative for the North of England in 1965, I had to give talks on its work. They could last for an hour, and therefore needed a lot of preparation for, of course, I cannot use notes. They have to be planned, recorded, edited, expanded, and memorized, and often I delete the whole of the first draft and start afresh. Far from being a chore, I find preparing these talks extremely satisfying. I've mentioned our concerts. They are quite separate from the talks, which are my main job. But, over the years, they have become part of the job as well, though, again, Alice and I have given concerts which have nothing to do with St Dunstan's at all. What often happens is that I give a talk to one group or another, and as a result we are invited back to give a concert.

Over the years Alice and I have fulfilled well over 3000 engagements on behalf of St Dunstan's — and she has driven over 350,000 miles! — so there's been plenty to keep both of us busy. We've performed in every conceivable location, before a wide variety of audiences, with professionals at the Mermaid Theatre in London and pensioners in village halls all over the North of England — and I shall have occasion to mention some of them later — and Alice has struggled through gales and snow, fog and flood, to get us there. And talking of floods, we were on our way to Halifax to give a concert, the rain was coming down in torrents, and there was water everywhere. We were just going

144

under a bridge when Alice stopped and pulled off to the side. There was two feet of water over the road, and I said to Alice and Winnie, who was with us, "Why's the car rocking? It's like being in a boat!" "We might as well be," Alice said, "it's up to the door-sills!" She managed to reverse out into shallower water, turn round and take another route. When we finally arrived at our destination we learnt that the River Calder had burst its banks, and our audience were quite surprised — and relieved — to see us. We were quite surprised and relieved to be there. Another time, when Alice was pounding down the M5 in the outside lane — she's a good driver and doesn't hang about — we had a burst tyre. The road was very busy at the time, but she managed to keep control, take her chance, and pull in on to the hard shoulder. She admitted afterwards that for a moment she had felt helpless — but not half as helpless as I did! For a former lorry driver it's not easy to sit there helpless while she does the driving, often in vile conditions, and she would no doubt accuse me of back-seat driving!

I'm digressing. There is one other source of pleasure and relaxation I can turn to, in the mornings or any other time, and that is the "Talking Book". With the multi-track tape adapted, again, by St Dunstan's, so that I can operate it by myself, I can have fifteen hours of uninterrupted reading — or rather listening. It's a wonderful service and is post-free through the British Talking Book Service for the Blind. I didn't, as you can imagine, get through a great deal of reading when I was young, so Talking Books gives me a chance to catch up.

I particularly like biographies — of Churchill, Mountbatten and Noel Coward, for instance — autobiographies such as Dirk Bogarde's and David Niven's and novels by writers like A. J. Cronin, Priestley and Richard Llewellyn.

I enjoy my early morning listening and learning in the familiar surroundings of my office, which I've never seen, but the day really begins when Alice is up and about to help me wash, shave and dress, and give me breakfast. And this, being the normal time for such events, brings me to the subject of toilets, a sensitive matter for all people without hands. Relief came when the late Air Commodore Dacre, when Commandant of St Dunstan's, discovered, somewhere in Europe, the *electronic toilet*. Air Commodore Dacre's other — and, as far as I'm concerned lesser — claim to fame was that, as a lieutenant in the Royal Naval Air Service at Gallipoli in 1915, he was the first man to torpedo a ship from the air. Such a feat, however, fades to insignificance when compared with the feat of introducing into Britain the magic loo. This splendid machine solves all our problems. At the required moment, at the press of a lever, a jet of warm water spouts up, followed by a stream of warm air. Super! Fantastic! As I tell my audiences — and it's always good for a laugh — I may not be beautiful, but I have a beautifully clean bottom.

"George," as the device is christened after its introducer, has since been installed in many disabled people's homes, sometimes only after overcoming opposition from the local water authorities, as it had an open valve, which used to be technically illegal. Anyway, it is a subject of lively interest to people from all walks of life, as I discovered at one of the annual Sportsmen's Nights which are held at the Players' Theatre in Villiers Street in London. The commentator was Harry Carpenter and the guest of Honour that year was Princess Anne. I was to be interviewed during the course of the evening, and beforehand Harry had a word with me.

"Any ideas what we might talk about, Billy?"

I thought for a moment. "Well, there's always my special electronic toilet. That usually gets a laugh."

Harry shook his head. "A bit close to the bone. How about swimming?"

"That's fine," I said.

I thought no more about it, but, later on, when I went up on to the stage, the first thing Harry said was, "Billy, I hear you have a rather unusual loo in your house. Perhaps you could tell us about it?" I could have died. There's all the difference between describing it to a bunch of Royal British Legion veterans and a posh audience with Royalty present. However, there was no escape, so I rattled on about it, and even mentioned the problem of power cuts, and it went down all right. Afterwards, though, Princess Anne came over to me and said with a chuckle, "That was fascinating, Mr Griffiths. I think I'll have to get one." But I've never had the chance to ask her whether she did or not!

As far as I'm concerned, it's one of life's more tiresome daily problems solved, and another little bit of independence for me, one less chore for Alice.

iii

As I grew more confident of my singing, and Alice and I became experienced duettists, the demands for us to give recitals increased, both locally and further afield. We joined the choir of Audley Range Congregational Church, which we always attended on Sunday mornings, and the minister, the Rev. J. E. Watson, used to ring me during the week with the hymn numbers so that I could learn the words. On special occasions I sang a solo. The organist, Ken Dewhurst, whose stepmother and sister had been interned by the Japanese, which formed a bond between us, used to rehearse me for these events. It all helped to increase my confidence, and kept me on my toes. Bobby was a member of the Scout Group at Audley Range, and we often took part in concerts to raise funds for their equipment. We sang for various charities, we sang in different churches, in hospitals, in homes for the elderly, and even in prisons.

As to the last of these, we were invited to give a recital in HM Prison, Lewes, not long before Christmas one year. There was a line in one of our songs which ran: "Bless these walls so firm and stout". I mentioned this, and suggested that the following line should go: "When you're in you can't get out". I thought the laughter would lift the roof off! A little time later we received two letters of appreciation from inmates, and I would like to quote part of the one from No 188338. After saying how much they'd all enjoyed our concert, and congratulating us "both as artist and citizen doing a wonderful job of work" — which, deserved or not, was nice — he wrote:

> My disabilities are so much smaller than your own have been. For mine are all self-inflicted. I am not blind, Bill, but I could not see the right and Christian way of life. Or worse still, I could see but closed my own eyes to it. I have two hands which in the past I have used as weapons of crime by stealing. Had I lived years ago could not I have lost both these precious hands for my deeds? . . . I thank you so much for what you have given me personally, by your own example of great strength under such hardship. I am now certain that my own determination to succeed in life cannot possibly fail.

I often wish I knew whether that man's resolution lasted and was strong enough to keep him straight when he came out, but, in any case, just to know that one had given him encouragement and the ability to see the error of his ways made it seem worthwhile. Over the years we have had many, many similar letters, not merely from prisoners and the bereaved but from all sorts of people whose troubles have been put in a new light.

Singers need an accompanist, and this is a good place to mention the two pianists — dear friends both — who have played for us so loyally over the years. Until 1974, when she retired, Winnie Fee came with us on all our concert engagements and put up uncomplainingly with long car journeys, large and small halls with dreadful acoustics, and, very often, with ancient, out-of-tune pianos. Since then her place has been taken by Ellen Rawcliffe, of whom exactly the same can be said. Ellen and her husband Ernest have supported and encouraged us — and indeed fortified us, for Ernest brews up a lovely drop of homemade wine! — and Ellen and Alice and I have become an inseparable team. Before each concert we have a rehearsal, either at their house or ours, and the combination of shared skills and warm friendliness continues to act like a tonic on me — and I don't just mean Ernest's three-year-old damson either. No, it's the feeling of "belonging", of being part of ordinary day-to-day life and not set apart as a "case" that is so important to the disabled. At first, and in a very different way, I was only able to feel this at St Dunstan's, when we were all "special cases"; but then, when Alice and Bobby and I became a real family, and after that, when Alice and I started giving concerts and meeting hundreds of different people all over the country and abroad, a whole new world opened up for me. And now, here I am, trying to write a book about my life! The frontiers which once seemed as narrow as a prison cell have become boundless.

Another thing that has proved a great source of strength is the lasting comradeship between those who were prisoners of the Japanese. I was originally encouraged to join the Manchester Far Eastern Prisoners of War Association by a parson friend, Ray Rossiter, himself an ex-FEPOW, and, as a result, I have served for the last ten years as honorary public relations and liaision officer for the blind. There are sixty-eight clubs within the Federation, in nine areas, each with its own chairman, secretary, treasurer and welfare officer, and every year there is an annual conference, with a national reunion in Blackpool every two years. There has always been a powerful sense of grievance among FEPOWs that their sufferings, and especially the long-term effects of malnutrition and disease, have never been properly recognized by the authorities; and exerting pressure through Parliament for a fair deal for all those whose health was permanently damaged or undermined by conditions in the camps has been one of the main objectives of the Federation. Welfare, another aspect of the same refusal by Government to take the necessary action, is another priority, with a central fund available to help those in need.[1] At the annual London FEPOW reunion, which until this year has taken place in the Royal Festival Hall — in 1988 it will be at the Barbican Centre — one meets dozens of old friends who shared, to a greater or lesser degree, the hardships and miseries of those years. Sadly, at each reunion more names are missing as age and illness thin out the ranks.

"I came specially to meet an old pal of mine," one will say, "and now they tell me he can't make it this year."

---

[1] As a result of pressure by the Federation, a special FEPOW unit was finally established within the Department of Health and Social Security.

151

One who did make it in 1987 was Sir Edward Dunlop, the man who saved the life of a good many of those present, including my own, and who, then as now, at the age of eighty, makes nonsense of his nickname of "Weary". On the Burma-Thailand railway, and in Java, in conditions worse than Florence Nightingale found at Scutari, he performed medical miracles, and acts of sublime courage, which no one will ever forget, and which send man after man to have a word with him.

"I remember him," one says, "operating inside this kind of mosquito net, and I had to make up drips using bamboo linked together with bits of stethoscope tube." And another, "This kempetai comes raging down the ward knocking the patients about with his bamboo staff, and Weary, he steps in front of him, takes the staff from him, breaks it across his knee, and says to this bastard, 'Now go away and be a good boy' — and *he does!*"

Weary was in England for the British publication of his *War Diaries*, illustrated with Jack Chalker's prison camp drawings, and before he went back to Australia he came to Blackpool to stay with Alice and me, a joy to us both. Alice, especially, has never forgotten the first time he came to see us. She was in the kitchen, cooking fish and chips, when there was this ring at the front door of our bungalow in Blackburn. "Oh —!" she says, "who can that be, ringing the bell at this time of night?", and she goes storming off to open it, still with her apron on, and this quiet voice says, "Mrs Griffiths? It's Weary Dunlop. May I come in? I'd like a word with

Billy." He and Lady Dunlop had come all this way north just to visit me, never let us know or anything, just found his way to our house, rings the bell, and asks if he can come in! We were bowled over, I don't mind saying. But that's Weary Dunlop, a man whose kindness and compassion are inexhaustible, yet whose sheer force of personality could quell the most brutal of Jap guards.

iv

Weary wasn't the only one of my ministering angels from POW camp to come and see me after I got home. One day in 1955 I was sitting in the lounge, concentrating on one of my "talking books", when I heard a deep, soft voice, with a slight accent, saying, "I must see Billy Griffiths". Thirteen years had passed since I had last heard it, but in that instant I was back in Bandoeng hospital, in utter agony and despair and crying out to be given a swift, merciful death, and that calm, gentle voice came through to me, trying to offer me comfort and courage, the voice of the Matron, Mickey de Jonge.

"Mickey!"

"Billy!"

I sprang out of my chair and rushed to the door, and she threw her arms round me.

"Wonderful!" she said. "You look fine!"

"And you?" I said. "Are *you* all right?"

"Yes, good, yes."

I hadn't even known whether she had survived, only that she had taken part in secret resistance work and had been caught by the Japs and tortured. And here she was, alive and well, in my own home. I couldn't believe it.

She wouldn't talk about that time, only that in the troubles that followed the end of the war when the Indonesians had taken over Java, she, like most of the other Dutch people, had had to leave, and she was now settled in Holland, and had found an opportunity to keep her promise to come and see me.

"And you, Billy? How have you been getting on?" I was able to tell her about starting my transport business, and how it had been going quite well until nationalization; and how, after I'd had to give it up and was in a very depressed and nervous state, Alice had come to my rescue, which was how I came to be a paying guest in her house, and how she had persuaded me to take up singing, and what a joy it was for me to have something active and absorbing to do instead of just sitting about all day listening to the radio and being taken out for walks.

"Wonderful, Billy," she said. "Perhaps I will be able to come and hear you sing."

"I shouldn't advise it," I said, and we had a good laugh about that.

"I was told about how you used to walk about in POW camp with a stick tied to your arm," she said, "singing. When I heard that, I knew you would be all right."

Mickey is in every way a remarkable woman. Very tall — I just about come up to her shoulder! — her father was the Minister for War in Holland and later Governor-General of Java; she had been educated with Queen Juliana at the Palace in The Hague. On her return to Holland after the war, Queen Juliana sent for her to get her opinion on what had gone wrong in Java. Mickey protested that she couldn't possibly come, as she was in rags. "Never mind," said the Queen, "I'll send a car for you." And go she did, as she was, in the tatters in which she'd been released. She has stayed with us several times since, and we've met both in London and Brighton, and keep in regular touch. Ironically, her own eyesight is now failing.

When she left I felt quite emotional, overwhelmed by memories, and deeply touched by her keeping her promise and coming to see me after such a long time. There are no words to describe what I felt, only that I felt happy and grateful, and very humble.

A few years later I had another visitor from the past, the third of that trinity of saints who helped me through the worst times — Andrew Crighton. He was the one who spent several hours each day picking the little bits of shrapnel out of my body, and who, in the kindest possible way, told me that my sight had gone for ever but that wasn't the end of the world. When we knew he was coming, Alice cooked up all sorts of exotic foods, which Andrew ate up happily. Only when he was leaving did he admit that he'd been waiting eagerly for bangers and mash and Lancashire hot-pot! He and his wife, Pam, came to stay with us in

Blackpool; we visited them in Florence, and, quite recently, we met her again in London. We had a good yarn about those old, bad times which we could now laugh about because they were all over. Andrew who, at that time, had been in RAF Intelligence, had joined the Consular Service after the war, and was living in Italy. He was in England, visiting relatives in Cheshire, and had gone to the trouble of finding out where I lived. I never saw him again, but we corresponded regularly, and one day in 1986 Pam asked us to write specially as he was dying. Apparently he enjoyed my letters, and had kept them all.

Talking of old friends and comrades from those far-off days, only recently I spent a few hours with my ex-POW colleague, Joe Gannon. Joe — that's what he used to call himself, but he now prefers his real first name, Ossy — was the only other blind man I ever knew in POW camp. He had lost his sight the day after me, in the same place, on the same job. He came from Wigan, which was another bond between us, and, as I said earlier, he and I used to wander round the camp together — a classic case of the blind leading the blind. Joe — I mean Ossy — also used to help me have a "shower", so-called; that is, he threw buckets of water over me — a case of the blind *washing* the blind! — though, as we had no soap, it was more of a lick and a promise than a proper wash. Neither of us had any money. Those who did were sometimes able, but only for the first few months, to buy a certain amount of food from the Javanese. When these transactions were taking place, he and I used to sit ourselves down nearby like a couple of beggars, which is what we were, in the hope that someone might feel sorry for us and give us a handful of nuts, an apple, or, if we were lucky, an egg. Sometimes it worked, too.

That's by the way. Talking over old times, remembering some of the characters we'd both known — the British RAF Dr Lillie, Father Elliott, the swearing padre, and others — and the grim future ahead, I realized for the first time that he had viewed it with exactly the same dread as I had, but, like me, he'd coped with it better than he'd expected. In his case, as in mine, it was St Dunstan's that had taught us to come to terms with blindness, though I'd been luckier in having Alice to help and encourage (and chauffeur!) me. Ossy had never been to a FEPOW reunion, and had never talked to anyone else about his experiences.

"Do you remember," I said just before we parted this time, "you and I were sitting outside late one night, not long before the end of the war, and we heard an aircraft going over very high, and you said firmly: 'That's one of ours', and soon afterwards we heard the bombs being dropped?"

"Ay, I do," he said. "It cheered us up no end, did that."

"It's over forty years ago," I said, "and here we are, still going strong."

"Ay," said Ossie Gannon, whom I would always think of as Joe, my old blind pal from POW camp.

In 1964 Mrs Elizabeth Dacre, the wife of the Air Commodore (of Blessed Memory) and at that time

157

Sussex County President of the Women's Section of the Royal British Legion, invited us to come and give a number of recitals in and around Brighton. This led to a whole series of further engagements, including my singing solo at the Remembrance Service at the Dome during their conference, something I did for many years. For a number of reasons Alice and I had been considering the idea of settling in the south, the climate, and nearness to St Dunstan's being two of them; so in that year we sold our bungalow in Blackburn and rented one from friends in Ovingdean who were off to spend six months in Australia. However, as soon as we started to look round for a suitable property of our own we learnt better. The price we'd got for our bungalow would just about have bought a hen-house down there. In any case, just before we'd left Blackburn, Bobby had married a lovely girl, Christine Walders, and they'd settled in Burnley, near the hospital where they both worked.

Our roots were in Lancashire, and even if it had been possible for us to move permanently to the Sussex coast, I'm sure the north would eventually have drawn us back. As it turned out we were soon presented with another, and quite different, indeed, rather exciting reason for returning.

For it was during that busy and interesting six months that I was given the opportunity of being taken on as a member of the staff of St Dunstan's as their speaker and public relations representative in the North of England. Although by this time I'd had quite a lot of experience of appearing in public at charity concerts and the like and had once presented the prizes on St Dunstan's behalf at some do or other, this was rather different. I'm not saying that Alice and I hadn't always given of our best, whatever the occasion, but we'd only been representing ourselves. If we, and I say "we" although technically I was the person who was offered the job, but for all practical purposes we were a partnership — if we were to appear on behalf of an organization, even one as tolerant and generous as St Dusntan's, there would inevitably be a stronger psychological pressure on us to be even better. There could be no excuses, even if it meant, as it did on one unforgettable evening, ploughing through a snowstorm to reach Consett in County Durham for an engagement.

It would be a challenge all right, but wasn't that exactly what I'd been seeking right from the start? A job of work, something I could get my teeth into, some responsibility. If I say I've been lucky — and I know that in a hundred ways I have been — I only need to state that Alice, who must have had a pretty good idea of what it would involve for her, supported me wholeheartedly. (If she'd known then what she knows now, she might not have done! Winter driving in the North is no joke.)

So, anyway, in August, 1965, having fulfilled our engagements in Sussex, we returned to Blackburn and I started work. Raising money for St Dunstan's, I was told, was not the first priority, though that was obviously part of it. The main object was to give as many people as possible some idea of what the organization was doing for blind ex-servicemen and women, and so to increase their awareness of the problems which blind people have to cope with. In my talks I do not ask for donations, and Alice and I prefer not to accept them on St Dunstan's behalf. If, at the end, the organizers have a whip-round — and usually they do — we ask them to send the proceeds direct to Head Office. Our job is to entertain and inform. I must say that I — we — have always had all the support and encouragement we could possibly want from the staff: from William Weisblatt, the Secretary, from David Castleton, the Public Relations Officer, the indispensable Miss Cynthia Mosley, the Northern Welfare Superintendent, and everyone else, both at Headquarters and at Ian Fraser House.

St Dunstan's, as I hope I've made clear, was founded for men and women who were blinded on war service during World War One, and its charter restricts it to helping those in the Services whose blindness is attributable to war service. This increasingly includes FEPOWs whose sight has deteriorated over the years as a result of the disease and malnutrition they suffered in the camps. In this it is different from the Royal National Institute for the Blind, and the many voluntary blind societies, which exist to help all blind people. But, since many of the problems are common, St Dunstan's and the RNIB work closely together, and I have on a number of occasions been asked to help both the RNIB and the voluntary societies as well.

Once I remember very well was in 1968, which was the Institute's centenary and was nominated "Help the

Blind Year". I was invited to give a series of talks at the Styal Prison for Women in Cheshire and, as a result, the inmates presented things which they had made, toys, cushions, etc, to be sold in aid of the Talking Book Service. They fetched over £70, and I received a nice letter from the Director-General of the RNIB in which he said I had "succeeded in raising the interest of the prisoners in blind welfare", and recorded his "heartfelt thanks for this particular effort and indeed for the fine work that you are doing in the North of England for blind welfare."

I hope that's true, for I believe it to be a thoroughly worthwhile cause. Only those who have lost their sight can know fully what a curse it is, but, unlike deafness, it does tend to find ready sympathy among the sighted; and if sympathy can be transformed into practical and active help, so much the better. I know from my own experience how much the organizations concerned[1] have done to let some light into the dark world of the blind, and promoting their cause is a way of saying thankyou.

To be both blind and without hands of course makes one a fully paid-up member of the disabled and means I can also draw attention to the plight of the many thousands of men and women who, either through war service or peacetime accidents, have lost limbs, and I felt deeply honoured when, in 1969, I was unanimously elected a Life Member of the Blackburn Branch of the

---

[1] Not least the Blackpool and Fylde Society for the Blind, of which I am a Council Member.

British Limbless Ex-Service Men's Association to which I had reluctantly paid my five bob all those years ago. In his letter telling me this, the Secretary, David Astley, mentioned particularly "donations received over the past years for which, directly or indirectly, you have been mainly responsible."

On the very same morning on which I received that letter I had another, equally gratifying, to say that I had been voted Disabled Sports Personality of the Year by the Sports Writers Association of Great Britain. I wondered then, and have often questioned since, how it came about that I was chosen for such honours: what had I done to deserve them? Nothing so special, it seemed to me, if in trying to make something of my life I had been enabled to give a bit of help and encouragement to others in the same boat. Still, I won't even try and pretend I wasn't delighted, and to find myself, a few weeks later, up on the platform with Ann Jones and Tony Jacklin, respectively sportswoman and man of the year, while we were presented with our trophies by Denis Howell, the then Minister for Sport, was amazing and exciting. During the course of the evening I was introduced to literally dozens of the outstanding sportsmen whose voices and achievements I knew by heart from listening to the sports broadcasts over the years, a tremendous thrill for someone as keen on sport as I am.

The climax of the evening came when they were all assembled at one end of the room for photographs and the TV cameras. Alice and I were at the top table and she whispered to me, "You ought to be there with them" in her determined way. It was almost as if someone had heard her, because at that moment the toastmaster called for silence and announced that the Chairman of the Sports Writers Association, Reg Gutteridge, would now escort Mr Bill Griffiths, "our Disabled Sports Personality of the Year" to join the others for the photographs. "There you are," Alice hissed as I got to my feet, "I said you should be there!" and Reg grabbed my arm and propelled me the length of the room.

When the photo-call was over, Tony Jacklin and Henry Cooper started an argument between them as to which of them was to take me back to Alice, and pretended to have a fight about it. I heard all this going on, to discover that Tony Jacklin had "won" and was my escort back. One way and another I couldn't help feeling a bit out of my class in such company!

If, like me, you listen to the radio a lot, and I daresay this applies even more to television, you become so familiar with certain people's voices you almost feel they're old friends, but it's still quite a thrill actually to meet them in the flesh, so to speak, as happened to me at the Sports Writers do. When you find out that this one or that comes from the same part of the world as you do, fame, stardom, call it what you like, suddenly becomes local and almost homely. Everybody knows that George Formby was a Lancashire lad. I'd loved his films, especially the pre-war "Up for the Cup" which I still remember vividly, and I'd actually talked to him just before I was posted overseas, when he sang at a show in Blackpool. So it was funny to be told, after a

163

talk I'd given at a school in Warrington, that there was a blind lady in the audience who wanted to meet me, and she was George's mother. So we were introduced, and I said something to the effect that she must be proud to have such a famous son. All she said, in a rich Lancashire accent, was, "'E's not a bad lad, George!" No one, they say, is a hero to their family.

On a quite different occasion I found myself sharing a platform with the Mayor of Blackburn and the television personality, Russell Harty. I had to make a few remarks, and I happened to say how amazed I felt to find myself in such illustrious company. There was nothing tongue-in-cheek about this; it is a source of wonder to me, and always will be. But this time I had the tables turned on me, which was even more surprising. A lady I didn't know came up to me afterwards and said, "I wouldn't have been here but for knowing that I might have a chance of meeting *you!*" Before I could find an answer to this, she went on, in a good homely Lancashire accent, "Our Russell told me you were coming, so I simply had to come!" It turned out that she was his mother and lived in Blackburn where the family were fruiterers and had known my grandfather. There's fame for you!

Other people are household names, famous in their different professions, and meeting them is much more alarming, at least in anticipation. The Duke of Edinburgh came to one of our FEPOW reunions in Blackpool, and I was presented to him. The conversation, which I remember very clearly, went like this:

The Duke: "What was your unit during the war?"
WG: "The RAF, sir."
The Duke: "Oh, shot down, I presume?"
WG: No, sir, blown up!"

I was to meet him again at various functions and always found him ready for a laugh.

Earl Mountbatten was the Guest of Honour at one of the Sportsman's Nights[1] at the Players Theatre one year, and I was introduced to him. I was able to tell him how I had met Lady Mountbatten on my release from POW camp, and how she had put new heart into me. Later that same evening I was squeezing past him to get back to my seat, after being interviewed, when I trod heavily on his toe. I started to mumble an apology and he said, "Ouch! You've put on some weight since your POW days, Griffiths" — something I couldn't deny.

During a charity concert rehearsal for RAF prisoners of war which Alice and I were involved in at the Mermaid Theatre in London, we were on stage having a run through with the pianist. Everyone else in the theatre was busy preparing for the evening show and taking no notice of us, with the exception of one man in the front row. During a break, Alice mentioned him to me. "It's a funny thing, you know, he's watching us all

---

[1] "Sportsman's Nights" are held at the Players Theatre each year, and have no connection with the Sports Writers' event mentioned earlier. Under the previous Chairman, Dorothy Taylor, Sportsman's Nights raised money for blind babies. Now, under Joan Rothschild, their beneficiaries are disabled sportsmen and women, and Alice and I attended them for many years.

the time. I do wonder who he is; he's ever so scruffy in his old pullover." We went on with our practice, and at the end Alice whispered, "He's coming over to us, that scruffy chap," and then I heard a voice say,

"Mr and Mrs Griffiths, how do you do? I'm Bernard Miles. That was grand." He stayed chatting with us for quite a long time, and then he turned to me. "You've got a good song there. Just "speak" it a little more." I knew exactly what he meant: it was what we call a "Point" song, in which the words need to be punched out clearly. Useful advice, and nice of him, I felt, to take the trouble.

I don't quite know why one should be surprised when famous people are civil to one, but one is! In fact, I can't remember receiving anything but courtesy and friendliness from any of the well-known personalities I've had the good fortune to meet, from dukes and duchesses to singers, actors and sportsmen.

One who was none of these things but a person for whom I've always had the deepest admiration is our former Mayor of Blackburn, Margaret McNamee. She has unquenchable courage and when, in 1967, she had to have a leg amputated, she never for a moment allowed it to interfere with her work for the community. Now in her 80's, she is still fighting for what she believes to be right. It was in connection with one of her causes that she originally introduced me to Barbara Castle, then our MP in Blackburn. The Chronically Sick and Disabled Persons Bill had just been passed, and Lord Taylor of Blackburn brought her to our home so that she could see for herself the problems of one

166

disabled person, and the various devices that helped to make life easier for him. One of the things I demonstrated was my adapted telephone. I pretended to dial a number, waited a few seconds, then turned to Barbara and said, "It's Mr Heath for you". She didn't forget that little joke, as I shall show later on.

But, going back to Margaret McNamee, she and I got ourselves in a right muddle once when she came to our house here in Blackpool. Her daughter and Alice went off, leaving us on our own. On our way upstairs to the lounge, she dropped her stick, which went rattling down to the bottom. With only one leg and no stick, she was unable to move and couldn't even turn round to tell me where it had fallen. I left her clinging to the bannisters and went down and started groping round for it. Finally I found it and managed to tuck it into my left armpit, climbed the stairs again, and in transferring it to her, managed to drop it again, and down it went. By this time we were both laughing so much we were practically helpless, but, in the end, we managed to crawl to the top with me supporting her as best as I could, and I got her into a chair. It was like a scene out of Laurel and Hardy; and if Barbara Castle had seen it, she might have got an unusual view of some of the problems of the disabled!

vi

In October, 1972, I was invited to give a speech at the London FEPOW annual reunion. We still used to drive to London in those days — we don't any more — and we set off from Blackburn in the morning in pouring rain which turned into a mixture of drizzle and fog by the time we got to Watford, so we were a bit behind schedule when we arrived at St Dunstan's headquarters where we were to stay the night. However, it didn't matter, because the only appointment I had that evening was to meet Harold Payne, the FEPOW National President.

When we'd settled into our room Alice said, "I must go out and buy some new gloves. I think you should have a bit of a lay down, you look done in, Billy. Do you feel all right?"

"I'm fine," I said. "Just a bit tired. I wouldn't mind coming with you."

"No, you stay and have a rest. I'll not be gone long."

So off Alice went, and I lay down on the bed and went over my speech in my mind, and maybe I dropped off, because the next thing I knew Alice was back and saying we had to go soon, and she'd arranged for a taxi. I knew she didn't like driving in London, so that didn't surprise me; but I thought she was fussing a bit, making me change my shirt and things, when we were only going to a pub.

Anyway, down we went and the taxi was waiting, and we set off. I, of course, hadn't a clue where he was taking us, and after a bit I wasn't too sure that the driver had either, because he stopped and said, "Sorry. I think I've gone wrong. I'll have to turn round."

It seemed to me that he was driving halfway round London, but at last he pulled up and said,

"Here we are." He opened the door for us, and as Alice took my arm, he added, "Good luck, sir." Friendly of him, I thought, but people often feel they should try and say something encouraging when faced with another's disability.

Alice pulled me along, and I thought I felt a tenseness in her which was unusual.

"Are we late?" I asked her.

"Come along, Billy," she said, and led me down what seemed like a passage, and into a room full of people, all talking. It was very hot and very noisy. Ah, I thought, this must be the bar.

"Can you see Harold?" I asked. Alice didn't reply, but at that moment he came over and said,

"Good to see you, Bill. Like a drink?"

"Very much," I said.

"Whisky?"

"And a drop of water, Harold, please."

He went off to get it and I remarked to Alice, "I can do with that drink. It's dreadfully hot in here."

At that moment Ted Coffey, the London FEPOW Club Chairman, joined us.

"Hullo, Billy. By the way, I'd like you to meet a friend of mine. Eamonn Andrews, Bill Griffiths."

Well, I knew that name, in common with most of the population of Britain, and I thought, "I wonder what he's doing here. Must have popped in for a drink. Perhaps it's his local." He gripped me by the shoulder and said,

"Very pleased to meet you, Bill. I'm told that you regularly tune in at home to our programme, *This Is Your Life*."

"Yes, I do," I said. "Very good." In fact, I'd never much cared for it. I'd always found it a bit embarrassing, tricking some poor bugger into appearing in front of the TV cameras and then facing him with all those people he hadn't seen for years; but I knew it was very popular.

What I didn't know was that the Thames Television cameras had been on Alice and me from the moment we entered the hotel and were on us then, and I still hadn't an idea what was coming next . . . But I think Alice should take up the story at this point:

Five or six weeks before that evening at the Clive Hotel I had a phone call from our son Bob and his wife asking us over to their place. We went, and when we arrived Chris said she and I were invited to a fashion show at the Keirby Hotel in Burnley. Well, I didn't mind. Bill was happy to stay with Bob and the children, so off we went, just Chris and I. "What kind of show is it?" I asked her, but she wouldn't say. "It's all right. You'll see."

We got to the hotel, and I couldn't see any sign of a show.

"It's all right," Chris said, and made for the lift.

"It's *not* all right," I said. "What's going on?"

But she wouldn't say, and, when we came out of the lift, there were two men waiting for us. They introduced themselves as Jack Crawshaw and David McFarlane, and led us along the corridor and into a private room, where one of them *locked the door*! I was properly flummoxed. Then the first one, Jack Crawshaw, said, "Alice — you don't mind if I call you Alice? — would you like a drink?"

"No!" I said. "Not until you tell me what all this is about." There was a pause. Then Jack said,

"We might as well get to the point right away. We've come to ask your permission for your husband to be the subject of *This Is Your Life*."

So that was it. I didn't know what to say.

"Ee," I said in my broadest Lancashire, "I don't know, I don't think Billy'd like that at all."

"Why don't you think he'd like it?"

"To be honest, he doesn't care for the programme. He's often said, 'Fancy bringing people on that they haven't met for thirty or forty years and expecting them to remember. It's not fair.'"

"What do you think, Chris?" Jack asked her. He'd obviously made an ally of her, for she said to me,

"Go on, Alice. Billy won't mind. He'll enjoy it once he's got over the initial shock."

I still wasn't a bit sure, but finally they persuaded me, and I accepted that drink. And I needed it, for after a bit of discussion, Jack said,

"Can you promise to keep it an absolute secret? Not to tell *anyone* except those actually involved? If Billy finds out even ten minutes before the show, it's off. I'm sorry to be so strict, but that's the whole point of the programme. It has to be a complete surprise."

171

My mind was in a whirl, and I was already regretting having allowed them to persuade me, for we aren't like an ordinary couple where the man goes off to work, leaving the wife on her own. Billy and I are always together. How on earth was I going to meet the researchers without him knowing? It would be impossible even to use the telephone, and anyway, he always answered it. It was one of the things he could do, like his typing and his tape recorder and his radio, and I'd always encouraged it.

"It'll be very difficult," I said, but Chris chipped in, "It will be all right, Alice."

"That's what you've been saying ever since we left."

"Jack and David can contact Bobby and me when they want to meet you, and we'll arrange something between us."

"Oh, very well," I said. "I'll do my best."

"Super," Jack said. "We'll be in touch again very soon."

Whew! What a responsibility! The next few weeks were really dreadful. I just about ran out of excuses for getting away from the house and Billy. Once, when I had to meet Jack and David and I'd told Billy I had a hair appointment, I got back to the house and he sniffed and said, "You didn't have a hair-do, then?" He's got a nose like a retriever, and he knew at once because he couldn't smell the spray, and I had to lie and say it had been cancelled at the last minute. It was like walking a tightrope with someone standing at one end with an axe, ready to cut it at any moment! Another time, I'd wangled it for Billy to spend the

172

evening with a friend of his because Jack and David wanted to come to our house to get the atmosphere and see all Billy's gadgets. So they came and had a look round and went off, and I thought everything was all right. But the moment he was back in the house he said,

"Who's been smoking?" We'd both given it up — or rather, he had, I'd never been a smoker — and he knew at once. He went into his study and said, "What were they doing in here?" I'd invented some story about a visit from an insurance man, but Billy wasn't happy. He knew at once if things had been moved, which is very important if you're blind. "Oh," I said, "I was busy and he must have just wandered in when I wasn't looking."

I got away with it, but it was like that for the whole time, right up to the last minute before we left for London. The FEPOW reunion was on the Saturday, and the original idea was for the programme to be done there, but then the producer decided it was going to be too difficult and brought it forward to the Friday, which meant there had to be a reason for us to go to London a day early. Harold Payne, who was in the secret, rang Billy and suggested they meet on the Friday evening in the Clive Hotel for a drink to discuss the speech Billy was to make at the reunion. When he'd rung off, Billy said to me,

"They're making a lot of fuss about this speech, aren't they? It's only going to last five minutes!"

"Perhaps Harold wants to discuss other things as well," I said.

"And this Clive Hotel," Billy said. "Have a look in the AA Book, Alice, and see if it's in."

Well, I knew it was a 4-star place, but I pretended to look and said, "No, it's not there, Billy."

"Oh, it'll be a pub, I expect. We shan't be there long."

Little did he know!

I drove down in thick fog — they didn't think to tell me that everyone else was going by train, first class, at the company's expense! — and booked us in at St Dunstan's. They wanted me to go to the hotel by myself first for a sort of little rehearsal, and that meant that once again I had to leave Billy. I tell you, I'd had about enough of subterfuges and finding excuses to go out by this time, and I was damn sure something was going to go wrong at the last minute. I persuaded Billy that he didn't look too good after the journey and he'd better lie down for a couple of hours while I went out to buy a pair of gloves I needed. He didn't like that, because he enjoys coming shopping with me, likes to sense the atmosphere even though he can't check on what I'm buying! — but he finally agreed, and I told the housekeeper that under no circumstances was he to be disturbed. *She* didn't like *that*. "Billy always has a cup of tea with me in the kitchen," she said crossly.

"I'm sorry," I said. "He's not feeling well and he's to be allowed to rest and not to be disturbed."

By this time my nerves were in shreds. I took a taxi to the hotel, and Eamonn was there, and Jack and David, and they showed me the set, and how Eamonn would join us in the bar and take us through, and where we were to sit and so on, and I dashed back to St Dunstan's where I now had to persuade Billy that he was quite recovered.

"I don't know," he said, sitting on the bed half-asleep. "I don't feel too good, Alice."

"Come along, Billy," I said, "you'll be fine."

At last I got him up and ready, him grumbling all the time that I was fussing him and why did he have to put on a clean shirt, the one he was wearing was fine, and why was I being so particular brushing his hair over his bald patch when we were simply going round to a pub for a drink, and so on and so forth.

The final thing of all was what I was to wear. I'd been told to put on a long dress, and I knew, a, that Billy would be aware of this as we got into the car, and, b, that he'd want to know why I was wearing a long dress to go to a pub! So I said to him, "I've forgotten to bring a short dress with me. I've only got the long one for the Festival Hall tomorrow night."

"Wear that," Billy says. "You can get a piece of string and tie it round you and tuck your dress over it!" Honestly, MEN!

A company car came to fetch us. Billy thought it was a taxi with a clueless driver, and we reached the Clive Hotel exactly on time, and with poor Billy not having the faintest notion of what he was in for. What a relief!

"That's great," Eamonn Andrews was saying, "because, as your wife Alice knows, we're planning to do a show right now. Tonight, Bill Griffiths, THIS IS *YOUR* LIFE!"[1]

How many times had I heard that phrase as he introduced someone or other at the start of that famous programme, and friends and relations and long-lost brothers and sisters were all brought together in total secrecy for the occasion. But now, as he said the words, "Bill Griffiths, This is your Life" my mind went momentarily blank, and I'm sure my heart missed a couple of beats. I heard Eamonn say, "Well, we've more surprises in store, Bill . . ." and I thought, it's a dream, they're having me on, there's been a mistake . . . but he was saying, "The cameras are already on us, and in the next room there's an audience waiting. So if you and Alice would care to join me, we'll go through there now," and I said to myself, keep calm, keep calm! But my pulse was racing, and I felt an air of unreality, as if it was all happening to somebody else. I'm sure that for the first five minutes or so, as I sat on the stage next to Eamonn, I was in a state of shock and I was nervously going over in my mind who on earth they could have rounded up to meet me. I could see it was going to be a bit embarrassing whatever happened — not because I'd anything to hide — how could I have? — but simply trying to remember voices and who they belonged to, and where we'd last met.

Through a sort of mental haze I heard Eamonn say something like ". . . a life in which, through sheer guts

---

[1] Quotations from the programme by kind permission of Thames Television Limited, courtesy of Jack Crawshaw.

and determination, you've managed to turn tragedy into triumph . . . people who know the true extent of your courage and achievement . . . first of all, former European Heavyweight Boxing Champion, Henry Cooper . . ."

Well, I knew where we'd met, at the Bloomsbury Centre Hotel three years before, when I'd been nominated Sports Personality, and he and Tony Jacklin had pretended to fight over the right to take me back to my seat. Henry said some nice things about me, and gradually I began to relax; perhaps this wasn't going to be so bad after all. But then he wheeled on four other famous sportsmen and women, all of whom I had met, of course; the pilot, Sheila Scott, John Edrich, Terry Neil, and one I knew well, Cliff Morgan, who always did the commentary on the annual Sportsman's Night.

Then I heard Eamonn say ". . . achievements that could never have been visualized by our next guest when he met you more than thirty years ago . . . he's flown 12,000 miles from his home in Melbourne, Australia, to meet you again now — Sir Edward Dunlop."

My goodness! Weary Dunlop, now one of Australia's most outstanding medical men, in demand all over the Far East for his administrative as well as his medical skills, and he'd made time to come to England, just for this programme, the man who'd saved my life not once but twice. I felt quite overwhelmed at the honour, and it was wonderful to be with him again.

Next came my two brothers, Robert and Alan. Robert said a bit about me teaching him to swim in the

Leeds-Liverpool canal — Alan never got a word in! — and then Eamonn introduced the swimming team I was in when we won the Bolton Challenge Cup for my school just before I left. There wasn't much for me to do or say except "My!" and "Just fancy, after all these years!" and things like that, for I could see it was turning into a kind of "Bill Griffiths Admiration Society", which was the last thing I wanted. They'd even traced an old RAF mate of mine, Bob Bell, whom I hadn't heard a dickybird from since Singapore; and he told some yarn about a camp concert and me getting so exasperated with a bloke singing "Beautiful Dreamer" like a donkey with the belly-ache that I went up on stage and tipped him through the window — untrue, of course! However, they then produced the poor lad himself, Harry Simmons, and he started to sing the same thing again, and maybe if there'd been a window handy I might have felt like doing it again!

Eamonn then sketched in the events leading up to the explosion, and brought Weary on again, who said some flattering things about me.[1] And there, in the audience, were half-a-dozen old Java POWs, though I couldn't see them: John Denman, Hugh Makin, Alboin Smith, Col. Maisey, George Cathercole and others, names from a past so distant and awful it seemed as if it had been another life — and there they all were. John

---

[1] What Sir Edward actually said was: ". . . by his own determination he gave other POWs the will to keep fighting for life, in a situation where lesser human beings would have given up." — our Bill is too modest to quote it. (Editor)

178

Denman I'd kept up with, and one or two of the others, but many I'd almost forgotten until this moment.

And so it went on. Lord Fraser said a bit, then Alice had her turn and talked about our singing, and lo and behold, there were Harry and Winnie Fee who'd set me on the road, and a bit later on, a recording of the choir of Audley Range Church where Alice and I sang, and where we got married. The biggest surprise of all was, in Eamonn's words, '. . . a very famous lady politician who once came in to meet you and asked to see your telephone . . . ' — Mrs Barbara Castle, at that time our local MP, and the Shadow Minister for Health and Social Security.

It was perfectly true that she had come to our house and asked me to demonstrate how I managed the telephone, and I had dialled a number and said, "You're through now. It's Mr Edward Heath for you." She told the story again now, and it got a good laugh.[1]

---

[1] After the jokes, Barbara Castle said: "The thing that always strikes me about Bill is that he radiates happiness, genuine, positive happiness . . . While I was there I just felt that perhaps in life there is some strange compensation, you suffer some terrifying blow like Bill had and you take a positive reaction to it and that goes on, amplified, so you go on radiating something all your life. And that's what I think about Bill." In the following year Mrs Castle was able to pursue in the House of Commons a suggestion by Bill that the National Sports Council should have a disabled sports man or woman on it, which it did not have at that time. As a result, and despite the hedging by the then Environment Minister, Eldon Griffiths, this situation was remedied.

The team had persuaded my mother to come down for the programme, as well as Bob, Chris and their two children, now grown up, Shaun and Kim; but they had kept the biggest surprise for last, the woman whose voice had soothed and consoled me during those first awful weeks in Bandoeng, Mickey de Jonge, OBE. How strange and wonderful to hear it again now, without that unending, dreadful pain throbbing in my arms, in a television studio in London where, at that time, I had never expected to be again.

And with that, and Eamonn's final line, "Bill Griffiths, This Is Your Life", suddenly the show was over. It hadn't, after all, been too bad; and the party afterwards, when I was able to relax and enjoy the company of all the old friends which the programme had gathered together, was great.

For weeks after the show I kept getting letters, many from FEPOW comrades, some of whom I thought had died in prison camp, others from widows of FEPOWs still yearning for information about their husbands, where and how they'd died and so on. I must have received a hundred and fifty such letters, and many of them were very moving, though there was very little I could add to what they already knew. Then there were hundreds of phone calls, most of them very friendly and nice, but, human nature being what it is, a number from people who were disappointed at having been left out or were indignant because so-and-so hadn't been included. By and large, though, it had been an exciting and rewarding experience because, as I've said before, the comradeship that was built up as a result of the shared experience of prison camp has been a great source of strength to me, as to many others — only witness the number who still come to our reunions year after year. It created a spirit which will only die when the last of us has gone.

One thing about that programme which I haven't mentioned was how it came to be put on at all. Some years before, a journalist, Lucia Green, had written an article about me, we had become friends, and she had said that if ever we needed help over publicity or anything, we had only to let her know. Well, it so happened that the Emperor of Japan, Hirohito, was due to pay a state visit to England, and Alice and I thought that there should, perhaps, be some reminder of what he'd been responsible for, so I got in touch with Lucia. "I'll see what I can do," she said; but instead of writing an article on the subject, she'd gone to Thames TV and put to them the idea of my being the subject of a *This Is Your Life* programme, which, after much humming and ha-ing, they agreed to. [Geoffrey Pharaoh Adams, another ex-FEPOW says, "We forgive, but we don't forget".]

vii

This Is Your Life wasn't the first time I'd featured in a TV programme, nor was it the last. A year or two before, a BBC producer, John Hosken, whose name, oddly enough, I'd heard for the first time the very evening before he telephoned, came with a small unit to make a ten-minute film, and really put me through the hoops. He had me out on the local playing-field running, in the baths swimming, in my office typing and telephoning, and in the lounge, singing — a full programme. And more recently I was featured in a BBC series called *Unlucky for Some* produced by Tony Broughton. Apparently it only takes three people to make a ten-minute film, but eighteen to make one to last half-an-hour.

This mob arrived at our house at nine in the morning and kept themselves, Alice, Ellen, the family and me on the go till six o'clock at night. It was bedlam, what with all those people milling about, the cameras and the lights and cables everywhere, and I spent the day in a daze. The producer had decided it would be a change to do a scene outside, with me going for a walk with my two grandchildren, Shaun, who was then thirteen, and Kim, who was ten. Shaun and I worked out a few little jokes to liven things up, but unfortunately the rain started to come sheeting down, after one joke, and all he said, in a dispirited way, was, "I'm wet through"! Dear Kim grabbed hold of my arm and asked, "Are you all right, grandad?" — to which the correct answer would have been, "No. I'm wet through too", though I didn't say it.

As you've probably gathered, neither St Dunstan's nor anyone else had come up with a satisfactory substitute for my missing hands. My "dress hands" in their brown leather gloves are nothing but dummies, while the crab's claws quickly proved to be more trouble than they were worth. The result is, of course, that Alice has to do the honours. She's very deft at it, but some things are easier to pick up and shove into my ever-open mouth than others, and she happened to mention on this programme that her particular detestations were peas, and chicken on the bone. She also remarked that when we're eating out anywhere together she much prefers a quiet corner where we can get on with it in comparative privacy.

Well, it so happened that the day after the programme went out I was due to speak at a Masonic lunch. That morning the secretary rang me up in a panic: not only, as guests of honour, were we to be seated slap in the centre of the top table, but the main course was roast chicken and peas. I assured him it didn't matter and that Alice was only talking about when we were alone; but I think, if he could have, he'd have put us out of sight in an adjoining room with a plate of bangers and mash!

It's strange when you think about it that, with all these various appearances in front of the cameras, I have never seen myself and have no real idea of what I look like, either to myself or others. I have a mental picture, of course, but whether it tallies in any respect with reality I have no means of knowing. The last time I saw myself in a mirror I was twenty-one. Now I'm sixty-seven, and I daresay I've changed a bit during the past 46 years. But, as another blind chap said to me rather sadly once, "At least you've *seen* Alice" — whereas he'd never seen the woman he married, for he was already blind when they met. Alice, I'm sure, hasn't changed at all from the time we used to dance together before the war!

Talking of the telly and things, some years after I'd been subjected to having my life displayd for all to see, in 1979 to be exact, Alice and I had planned to go on holiday to Italy, where we were to stay with Andrew Crighton and his wife Pam near Florence. Everything was arranged, and we were just about due to leave when the phone rang one morning. I answered it and said, "Bill Griffiths here," and an Australian voice asked me,

"Mr Griffiths, does the name Weary Dunlop mean anything to you?"

"It certainly does," I said. "Why?"

"I understand he cared for you when you were wounded in Java; is that correct?"

I assured him that it was and he went on to ask me a lot more questions about my time in No 1 Allied General Hospital, Bandoeng, which I answered. That seemed to satisfy him, for he then said,

"My name is Brian Davies and I'm speaking to you from Sydney, Australia." My immediate thought was, "I'm glad you're paying for the call, but he went on, "We're doing a *This Is Your Life* programme on Sir Edward, and we'd like you to be one of the guests on it. Would you agree?"

"Yes, I'd be very glad to," I said. My next thought was, it'll cost the earth, but what did that matter against the prospect of being with Weary again? At which point Brian set my mind at rest by saying that Channel 7, Australian TV, would pay for the whole trip.

"You know my wife Alice will have to accompany me?"

"No problem."

So it was settled, and, as they didn't want us there for a couple of weeks, we were able to stay with Andrew and Pam after all. In the middle of it a film crew appeared to take some pictures of us all together, and at the end we flew straight on to Sydney, where we were met at the airport and given VIP treatment, 4-star hotel and all. And who should be there as well but Mickey de Jonge, who had been flown from Holland the day before.

What a reunion it was. After the programme, which was on the same lines as the British version, with Mickey and me being allotted two minutes each, Weary stayed on for three days and Mickey for a week, and in those somewhat happier circumstances we talked of the past and friends who had died in prison camp, and of friends who had survived, and the memories came flooding back. There in Sydney that time I met again one of the two other Australian doctors who were present when I was carried in more dead than alive, Major Ewan Corlette.

"Hullo, Bill," he said when we met, "how's the leg getting on?" He knew all about it, for he had apparently helped Weary sort out what was left of me. I was able to thank him for doing a good job. The other doctor in Bandoeng at that time was Major Arthur Moon, who had often come round and talked to try and comfort me. He, however, had recently died. At the end of the week, a week of great happiness and fabulous Aussie hospitality, we were taken back to the airport and put on the plane for home. It had been like a return match for Weary's appearance in my *Life*.

viii

What I haven't mentioned in relation to that trip was that Alice had one hand in plaster. It happened like this. We were out for a stroll one evening along the Promenade opposite the house — we'd moved from our home town to Blackpool a few years before — when she slipped and, in trying to save herself, had fractured a bone in her hand. She was in considerable pain, so we took ourselves to the local hospital, where they X-Rayed it, bandaged it temporarily, and sent us home in an ambulance.

I was climbing aboard when the ambulancemen discovered the state of their "passenger", after which they spent all their time looking after me at the expense of the "patient". So much so that when we arrived home the pair of them escorted me in and left her inside the ambulance till she shouted, rather plaintively, "What about me!"

With only one working hand between the two of us we might have had some problems, but I rang Bobby, and he and Chris and the kids jumped straight in the car and came over, arriving at midnight. Driving through the darkness on an "emergency" really thrilled the children, and they tumbled out of the car in a state of high excitement. We spent a week with them and then for the next two months managed on our own, with occasional help from friends and relatives.

One of the friends was Steve Cairns, FEPOW National Welfare Adviser. He came over one evening and had the job of helping me undress for bed. We'd got down to basics and he was struggling to get me into my pyjama trousers, when he suddenly exclaimed in mock amazement, "By! 'E's got one! I must tell the lads!" I had to point out to him rather firmly that I still had *some* of my — er — "appendages" intact!

The reason we'd moved from Blackburn, which is hilly, to Blackpool, which is flat, was because Alice had not been too well, and her doctor had recommended that she should take life a bit more easily. Also the sea air would be good for both of us. Although it was rather a wrench to leave the town which had been home for both of us all our lives, we both knew the south shore well. Exactly opposite where we moved to is the beach where I'd spent many hours as a child. (I'd also marched past it many times as an RAF recruit, but that's different.) The main thing is that, just like my old home town, although I cannot see it, I have a picture of it in my mind and, when the wind is off the sea, bringing that unmistakable seaweedy smell, it gives me a feeling of security, of knowing where I am, as well as good memories of my childhood. Memories made even more vivid when the grandchildren come over and we paddle and swim together and stroll arm in arm along the sands or on the "Prom". It's hard to explain, but sometimes it's almost as if everything that has happened in the last fifty or sixty years is momentarily wiped from my mind and I'm a child again, enjoying the sun and the sand and the sea with no thought for the future — which is now my past.

Another bonus for me was that many Blackpool men, including the entire Blackpool regiment, had been among those who had been captured by the Japanese, and so there is a strong FEPOW contingent here, with many relatives of ex-POWs, and an active association. At the same time the Royal British Legion is extremely good at looking after the interests and welfare of all ex-Service people and I was pleased to be invited to become the President of Blackpool South branch. Oddly enough, I was on the beach with Kim when the then Chairman, Harry Wilson, saw us and came over and "popped the question" — past and present mingling with a vengeance.

The British Legion is just one of the hundreds of organizations to which we have spoken, sung, or presented films over the years. I've already mentioned some of them, like the prisons, ex-Service reunions of all kinds, many Senior Citizens clubs, Rotarians and so on, and it would be boring, as well as impossible, to list them all, though in the list are both Eton College and Rugby School. We have rarely refused an invitation, even when it wasn't directly connected with the work of St Dunstan's, and more often than not the result has been a request to come and talk or sing to this group or association or that. One of the most unexpected came from the Women's International Zionist Organization in Bramhall in Cheshire. Alice and I duly went — to find that the reason for the invitation was so that they could present me with a certificate stating that a tree had been planted in Israel in my honour, numbered and with my name on it. I felt very honoured and, although I'm afraid I've never had the opportunity to go and inspect it — a fruitless exercise for me in any case — a few days later the local paper came out with a headline: 'Bill Griffiths: This Is Your Tree'! Somebody must have chuckled to himself when he thought of that.

A rather more sombre occasion was the Dedication Service to mark the restoration of the family tomb of the Dacres in Hurstmonceux Church in Sussex. Mrs Elizabeth Dacre, who is the sister of the late Lord Fraser and the widow of the Air Commodore, besides being a great friend of ours, had asked me to sing "Be still, my soul", and we were just going up to sing when I felt a tap on the shoulder, and a voice said, "Billy, I'm John Denman. Do you remember me?"

I did indeed. It was he who had rigged up an operating theatre for Weary Dunlop at Bandoeng — which the Japs had promptly demolished — and who had seen the mess I was in when I was carried in. I had had occasional letters from him, but this was the first time we'd met since that time, and after the service we had a long, deeply emotional conversation about those grim times.

John is one of those extremely concerned and sympathetic people, and he brought both his concern and his sympathy to bear on me later, with almost magical effect. Alice and I were about to move house, and as that's an operation in which I am more hindrance than help, I had retired to St Dunstan's to keep out of the way, and promptly fell ill. Dr O'Hara, who looked after St Dunstaners at Ian Fraser House, diagnosed it as being nothing more desperate than "Thrush", an infection of the throat, but its effect on me was devastating. I was thrown straight back to my days in prison camp when I'd had no interest in anything and all I'd wanted was to stay in bed. Ever since the war I, like most FEPOWs, had suffered from regular bouts of malaria, dengue, which is sometimes known as "breakbone fever" because of the ghastly pain in the joints which goes with it, high temperatures, and nightmares. But this deadly lassitude was as bad as anything I'd known. Alice was so worried that she abandoned her packing up and drove down. I just lay there, not so much physically ill as drained of all interest and all effort. In desperation, after a week of this, she said out of the blue, "Would you like to have a talk with John Denman?" I suppose I said yes, and John, who lives at Patcham, not far from Brighton, came straight over, although he had troubles of his own at the time.

He sat by my bed and we talked and talked — of our time together in prison camp when he had told me of the houses he hoped to build — he's an architect — after the war; of the awful times, and the few good ones; of anything and everything; it was as if he was drawing the poison of the past out of my system. From the time of his visit I began to pick up. There's no doubt that many, perhaps most, FEPOWs are specially vulnerable when they get ill, their resistance permanently lowered by malnutrition and disease. In the same way,

190

many who appeared to have recovered their health died in their 50s.

ix

Not all our concerts have gone smoothly. Harry Fee, who was a perfectionist, used to take endless pains rehearsing me beforehand, pulling me up if I was off pitch, correcting my pronunciation and so on; but there was little or nothing he could do about the pianos he had to play at the various halls where we were to perform. We would arrive, be met by the organizer and taken in to where the audience was waiting, all agog for the show. But Harry had eyes only for the piano. "Hmm!" he would murmur doubtfully, or "It looks all right, Billy". Then he would have a quick run up the keys. It might pass muster; it might be quite good, or it might be quite dreadful, and Harry would turn to the organizer and say in his sternest voice, "You know where this instrument belongs? On the bonfire!" Consternation all round; but, having made his opinions perfectly clear, Harry would proceed to play as well as the state of the piano allowed, which was invariably very well indeed.

On one memorable occasion, though, his lapse from perfection was not the fault of the instrument. We were giving a concert somewhere in Yorkshire, and towards the end his playing suddenly became so erratic that I thought he must have been taken ill. Alice and I were giving a duet at the time, and we struggled on to the end, although the audience, who had been quiet and

191

attentive, had started shuffling and talking. It was all totally puzzling to me, though not to anyone else: there had been a power-cut and the hall had been plunged into darkness!

I don't know if you can call this one of the very few occasions when being blind is an advantage, but the only other one that comes to mind occurred one evening when I was in the Comrades Club, standing near the bar with Reg Dunne, National Vice-President of FEPOW, and a voice said,

"Have a drink, Bill?"

"Thanks," I said, "I'd like a small beer," only to discover that he hadn't been addressing me but some other Bill. However, he did the decent thing and got me one.

This business of identifying voices, and trying to place where they're coming from, can be extremely tiresome. I am at a do of some kind, people milling about, voices, background music. I feel a tap on the shoulder. "Bill, good to see you. How are you?" "Very well, very well indeed," I reply, ransacking my memory. "Come on, Bill, you know my voice." I do, do I? Er . . . um. I should say straight out, "No I don't," but, afraid of hurting their feelings, I tend to mutter, "It rings a bell . . . lot of noise in here — can't quite get it." "It's John, Billy." John? John *who*? Probably somebody who invariably says of himself, "Never forget a face, just can't get the name." I don't have any faces to forget, unless I saw them before the 16th of March, 1942 — and that's forty-six years ago. (At the same time, I *can* put a name to most voices, sometimes to the amazement of the speaker.)

And anyway, *where* is he? Is he beside me, in front of me, hanging from the ceiling? I don't know, how can I? Where am *I*, come to that? Somebody towed me across the room, introduced me to some friends of theirs, stayed chatting for a bit, then moved away, leaving me on my own and completely disorientated. Over the years I've learnt to be patient and wait quietly until someone, usually Alice, bless her, comes and rescues me.

People are so different. Some seem to understand instinctively one's limitations, are there when they're needed, but don't fuss. Some treat one as if one were an idiot, and deaf into the bargain, while to others the fact that one has a few small problems — like recognizing voices or knowing where one is — doesn't seem to occur at all. And some people, of course, haven't the faintest idea what they're up against, and that can be embarrassing for both of us.

Until a few years ago, when I began to have a lot of trouble with them, I always kept my artificial eyes in during the day and once I was alone in the house when the front door bell rang. I went and opened it — it has a lever handle — and I heard a voice saying,

"Good morning, sir. Can I interest you in this really excellent range of men's shirts? An absolute bargain. Just look for yourself at the style, the cut, the bold but discreet patterns . . ."

"I'm sorry," I said, "I can't see them. I'm blind."

"Oh dear," he said. Then, undaunted, went on, "In that case, just feel the quality of the material, sir . . ."

"I can't feel it either," I said. "I'm sorry."

"Oh my goodness!" he said, gathered up his goods, slammed his case shut and bolted.

Another time the door bell rang and I went to the door and opened it. I stood there, not a word.

"Can I help?" I said.

No answer. "Can I help you?" I said again.

No answer, only footsteps retreating rapidly down the path and the garden gate shutting. Alice was upstairs and I called her and said,

"Who on earth was that? I asked him, or her, what they wanted and they never uttered."

Alice didn't know; and it was only later that we discovered that he — it was a man unknown to us — was both deaf and dumb! He didn't know I couldn't see. I didn't know he couldn't hear or speak. End of conversation!

And just to round off this catalogue of misunderstandings, there was the time when we'd arranged for our insurance agent to call round in the evening to collect our annual cash premium. Then Alice had to go out unexpectedly. "But I've left everything on the table in the lounge, all ready. Just let him in and tell him where to find it."

Off she went, and sure enough the doorbell rang and I answered it. "Come in," I said. "Everything's ready for you."

There was a pause, and then a very nervous voice said, "Would you mind turning on the light, sir?"

Only then did I realize, first that it must have been pitch dark, and secondly, that this was a new chap who'd never been to the house before and didn't know what to expect. A mugging, perhaps.

There was one other incident I remember which had the elements of farce. I'd been chief guest at the mayoral banquet in Blackpool, and after it the Mayor dropped me a line of thanks. I replied that it had been a pleasure, and added without thinking that during the coming Sunday Parade and March Past I would be giving him a smart "Eyes Right". Only after posting the letter did I remember that the saluting-base near the Town Hall was on the left, not the right; so I arranged with my escort to see that I was on the left side. Meanwhile the Mayor, in the light of my letter, arranged for the salute to be taken on the right — but nobody got round to telling me. Everyone out of step except our Bill!

So it goes, and as long as one can laugh about these things no harm's done.

X

In 1969 — this is going back a bit — I was invited to take part in the European Disabled Games being held in South Britanny. I entered for five events, the 100m breaststroke and the 50m backstroke, the 100m sprint, throwing the javelin, and the shot-put. Although I won no medals, the meeting was not without its comical side as far as I was concerned. In the first swimming event I was competing against a German, a Swede and a

195

Belgian and got a fairly good start, but half way I felt my trunks slowly but inexorably slipping down. At the end of the pool, as I turned for the final length I could feel them finally sliding over my hips, and I had the alarming experience, alarming for them, at least, of presenting to the throng of spectators lining the side, as well as about ten million viewers on TV, the spectacle of my bare bottom. Lucky it wasn't the backstroke!

For the track races the organizers brought the bed patients out from the adjacent hospital and lined them up on either side. Not a good idea, as the blind like to have plenty of space when they're running to allow for wandering off course. Each competitor ran separately and was timed. My turn came, I was lined up and set pointing in the right direction by my helper, who then ran behind to yell directions at me if I drifted. The pistol fired and away I went to the cheers of the multitude. I was doing rather well and the cheers grew louder — so loud, in fact, that I didn't hear my helper shouting STOP! The next thing I knew I'd run full tilt into one of the beds and gone arse over tip over it and its occupant, who, I was reliably informed, was a gorgeous, if at that moment rather shattered, blonde. She wasn't half as shattered as I was! No great damage, a few bruises, that was all, but for a long time afterwards, whenever I was about to take part in a similar race, I had a nagging anxiety that there might be some obstacle alongside the track into which I should surely go crashing. Blondes in bed notwithstanding, I prefer a clear run.

Incidentally, though nothing to do with this meeting, I took part in a sponsored swim on one occasion and covered a mile. This got into the papers and soon afterwards I had a letter from a complete stranger, asking me to meet him in London to discuss a project he had in mind — no less than that I should swim the Channel! He seemed to think, one mile, twenty-two miles — what's the odds? I thought otherwise and we did not meet.

Ever since the First World War the Royal Navy has taken upon itself to entertain fifty blind ex-Servicemen for a week each year at Lee-on-Solent, and this is now undertaken by the Fleet Air Arm. Each man has a sailor to act as his "guide-dog", and they look after us magnificently. In addition, they act as our escorts on special occasions, as for instance at the Remembrance Day parade. To three of these chaps in particular, John Scott, Gordon Brown and George Gilholm, I owe a great deal in the way of help and friendship. They were on hand when I went with the St Dunstan's team to Brittany, and during all the years — nearly twenty — in which I took part in the Disabled Sports at Stoke Mandeville, St Dunstan's, and at Lee-on-Solent, they were there. Earlier I mentioned Sir Ludwig Guttman, the Director of Stoke Mandeville Hospital. It was largely owing to him that I persevered with my various sports, for, after my first appearance at their sports, he said to me, "Great effort, Bill. Keep coming!" And I did, until a few years ago.

Inevitably Alice and I are often invited to take part in concerts and other functions intended to raise money for this good cause or that, quite apart from our work for St Dunstan's. In the case of Stoke Mandeville, our efforts were directed to selling symbolic "bricks" to raise funds to build a sports stadium. A contribution of so many pence or pounds would buy so many bricks. And in the early days, in fact during the time we spent in Sussex when we thought of trying to live permanently in the south, Mrs Dacre asked us to help her with a charity concert to be held at the Dome in Brighton to raise money for the Churchill Memorial Fellowship. We weren't to sing, merely stand on street corners distributing leaflets. The chief guest was Winston Churchill's grandson, "Young Winston" who, we were told, had expressed a desire to meet us.

Nothing more was said, the concert ended, the audience left, and we left them. We'd just got home when the phone rang. It was Mrs D., very cross. "Where are you? You were supposed to meet Mr Churchill and his family after the concert. They waited for ages for you!"

"We weren't told anything about it," Alice said, "except that he wanted to meet us. We thought the idea had been dropped."

Black mark for the Griffiths! However, some years later Winston Churchill and his wife were in Blackpool for the Conservative Party Conference and took the trouble to come and see us, which, under the circumstances, was very civil of them. The Brighton incident was forgiven and forgotten. They had merely wanted to thank us for our efforts on behalf of the Fellowship. They spent the afternoon at our house and were very pleasant, examining my various gadgets and asking us about our work for St Dunstan's.

Talking of gadgets, I don't think I've mentioned the one that most people find fascinating, and that is my wrist-watch. It looks like any other watch, but the glass is on a hinge and opens when I work the catch with my teeth. The dots on the face are raised and I can "read" the time with the tip of my tongue. On one occasion I was demonstrating my party trick to the Duke of Edinburgh and he asked me to tell him the time. Quick as light I flipped back the glass and said, "Ten past." "Ten past what?" asks His Royal Highness, so I told him. As I'd discovered on an earlier occasion, he doesn't let you get away with anything!

One last story about gadgets. The year I won the Electronic Rifle Shoot at the St Dunstan's Handless Reunion the story was picked up by a journalist who wanted to do an article about me for an American magazine. He came to see me, did the interview, and then said he wanted a picture of me with the rifle. This happened to be in Brighton, and we were in Blackburn. Not to be deterred, he managed to borrow an ordinary rifle and dragged me out into the park where he set me up with my artificial hands in the correct position, and the rifle levelled and aimed directly at the path which crossed the park. The journalist was setting his camera and at that moment an old gentleman, out for his afternoon stroll, happened to look our way — and found a man with a gun aiming straight at him. The journalist roared with laughter and the old gentleman moved faster than he'd probably done in the past twenty years. He was hardly to know that the gun wasn't loaded, I couldn't see him, and I had no means of pulling the trigger. I've no idea what the photograph looked like.

xi

1977 was the year of the Queen's Silver Jubilee, the year Princess Anne produced a son, and, incidentally, the year in which I was summoned to Buckingham Palace. This had nothing to do with Princess Anne's baby — though the two events did become slightly tangled up with each other — but something to do with the celebrations, for in the Queen's Birthday Jubilee Honours List it was announced that I had been awarded the MBE. That certainly made it a year of celebration for me.

I was notified in advance by the Prime Minister's Office, and when Alice opened the official-looking letter and read it out, I could hardly take it in. Surprised, amazed, delighted, all of those and a few more. "For Services to the Community", it said. My first thought was that, if that was true, it should have been awarded to us jointly, but I don't suppose they do that. Anyway, there it was in black and white, so Alice assured me, and read it again. "The Prime Minister is glad to inform you that Her Majesty the Queen has been graciously pleased . . ." or words to that effect. The Investiture was to take place in November and full instructions would follow. I was to present myself in top hat and tails at the side door of the Palace at half past ten on the 15th, and the ceremony would take place at eleven o'clock precisely. On arrival, we should be met by an attendant who would look after us.

Well! As the late Sid Field used to say, "*What a performance!*" Glad rags to be hired for the occasion — I couldn't imagine what I should look like in a top hat and, perhaps mercifully, I shall never know; a new suit for Alice, of course; arrangements with Bobby and Chris who were to come with us; a mounting sense of excitement; and a wish deep down that somehow the award could be shared with other St Dunstaners, and with my fellow ex-POWs who had been through the same experiences that I had. In a way I felt I was being given it on their behalf as much as on my own.

And so the great day came at last, cold but bright and sunny, Alice said, and off the four of us went in a posh hired car; not past those familiar railings and the sentries in their boxes but through the great iron gates and round the side entrance as instructed. I couldn't see it, but I could picture it vividly in my mind, so far, at any rate. After that I had to rely on Alice's description: the red-carpeted hallway, up in a lift, along a wide corridor which runs parallel with the balcony where the Royal Family make their appearances on great occasions, and into a small side room where we were to wait.

We had it to ourselves and Alice said, "I'd better put your eyes in now, Billy." They'd been giving me a lot of trouble, getting sticky and oozing, and we had decided to postpone putting them in until the last minute so that I should be "presentable". Normally this operation took just a few seconds, but now, in her nervousness, Alice dropped one of them, and could we find it! Bob and Chris were down on their hands and knees. Alice was rummaging about in the furniture — no sign of it — when an official came to see what on earth we were up to! "Well," Alice said, "you can't meet the Queen with one eye, you'll be better with none!" And then it was found, in the place where money and keys and spectacles and the children's marbles and everything else ends up, down in the depths of the settee. So we dusted off the fluff and in it went. Panic over.

We knew the Investiture was due to start at 11 o'clock. I kept on flipping open my watch and checking on the time: ten to, five to, eleven, five past, ten past. "She'll have been called to the hospital for the birth of Princess Anne's baby," Chris said. "I'll bet you." At that moment I was escorted into a side room and somewhere a band struck up some light music. One of the attendants came to me, attached a hook to the lapel of my coat, and said, "I shall escort you to Her Majesty. You will take ten steps, you will then stop and bow. At that point you will be directly in front of Her Majesty and about a foot and a half away, and she will attach the medal to the hook. Is that clear?"

"Quite clear," I said, with a lot more confidence than I felt. Inside, I was trembling with excitement tinged with anxiety and a tiny sense of disappointment that I should be there, face to face with the Queen, perhaps talking to her, and not be able to see her.

The music stopped. There was a rustle, a sudden hush, and they struck up the National Anthem. The last notes died away and Her Majesty said in her clear voice, "I am sorry to be late. The reason is that my daughter has just given birth to a son." Everyone clapped and then the investiture began.

One by one the names were called out by the Lord Chamberlain.

"Mr William Griffiths!"

I felt my arm firmly gripped: ten steps, the pressure on my arm brought me to a halt. I bowed. I could feel her presence. She said quietly,

"I am very glad you are here this morning, Mr Griffiths," and she shook my gloved hand with great vigour.

"I am delighted to be here, Your Majesty," I said and I felt her hooking the medal firmly to my lapel.

Then she asked me about my work, and I told her about the Royal British Legion, St Dunstan's and the Far East Prisoners of War Association, and taking part in sports, adding, after a moment, "for the disabled, of course." This made her laugh, and she said, "I know the Royal British Legion. That's wonderful. Thank you, Mr Griffiths."

It was all over. My escort turned me round and marched me to where the family was waiting, and we were taken back the way we had come.

Outside, photographers, television cameramen, and friends and relatives — including Kim and Shaun — of those who had been honoured were all jostling about. We were pounced on by a television team, and I just about managed to say how happy and proud I felt, etcetera, before Alice got going on the subject of the royal baby and how pleased the Queen looked and so on and so forth, and I never got another word in. And that, apparently, was what they transmitted that evening: me standing mute, facing in Alice's direction, and her rattling on about the "Happy Event" etc. That's what I meant when I said the two events got slightly tangled up. *WOMEN!*

It called for a celebration, anyway, and we all went off, Alice and I and Bobby and Chris and the children and David Castleton, my boss at St Dunstan's, for lunch at the Goring Hotel, and, all of a sudden, as we walked across Green Park in the crisp November air, I felt almost overwhelmed with happiness and gratitude for what life, fortune, God, had given me in return for all that had been taken away from me. Luck is more than winning the Pools.

Three years after this great occasion, in June, 1980, I received an honour of a very different kind, but one which meant as much to me in its way as being awarded the MBE. The Royal British Legion Housing Association had commissioned a small block of flats for ex-service men and women — elderly couples or those left on their own — in Blackburn and, in a gesture which I found very moving, decided to name it after me. "William Griffiths Court" it's called, and, since it was named after me, I had to open it.

This wasn't simply a matter of cutting a tape. The RBL laid on a parade, with 24 standards, and the band of the Lancashire Fusiliers playing what has become known as the *Bridge over the River Kwai* march,

"Colonel Bogey", and sounding Reveille and the Last Post, and a ceremony taken by four local clergymen. This was followed by a "do" at the Mill Hill Hotel, Blackburn, at which I was presented with an engraved silver tankard, and Alice a pendant and chain and a bouquet. In addition, the Housing Committee responsible for running the building gave us a silver dish.

Everyone was there. The High Sheriff of Lancashire, the mayors of Blackburn and Blackpool and their deputies, and representatives from all the organizations and associations with which I had been involved over the years, including St Dunstan's, the FEPOWs, the Burma Star Association, and others too. It was very much a Blackburn occasion; not quite "Local Boy Makes Good", but certainly for me a very special honour. Ernest Rawcliffe, who is the Chairman of the Housing Commitee, wrote in the *St Dunstan's Review* that "The naming of this building is a fitting tribute intended to ensure that the RBL remembers him with warmth and affection". I certainly felt both very strongly that day. Warmth and affection: who could ask for more?

xii

You might think, after what I said earlier about returning from the Far East and travelling blindly but yearningly across India in the train, longing to see for myself the countryside we were passing through, the busy, bustling streets of Madras and Bombay and all the rest of it, that I should have no interest in going abroad and no wish to do so. Perhaps, left to myself, this would have been so. All travel for me is a journey by night with the blinds down, an endless tunnel. But circumstances have changed since those early days, and so, I suppose, have I.

Of course I miss not being able to see. Who wouldn't? But as I said to someone who was sympathizing with me not long ago, "I've been without hands for forty-six years and I don't think about it." The same is true of sight. Once I'd come to terms with the facts of being blind and without hands I realized there was no alternative but to make the best of things; and the best of things for me has been meeting old friends and making new ones. That, not the scenery, is what has made travelling worthwhile. Quite apart from the journeys which Alice and I have made the length and breadth of England, during every one of which we have been warmly welcomed at our destination, we have now travelled widely abroad, and look like going on doing so for as far ahead as we can see!

I've mentioned our first trip to Australia to take part in Weary Dunlop's programme, and the joyous reunion with Mickey de Jonge. That was in '79. Five years later our friends Keith and Margaret Gledhill took us to Manchester Airport at the end of September bound this time for Melbourne and a great reunion of Far Eastern Prisoners of War. I must admit that, as I wrote in the *St Dunstan's Review*, "I wondered whether the long journey would be worthwhile. Would I meet many of those humorous, understanding, ever helpful FEPOW colleagues who had meant so much to me, as indeed the Dutch and British lads had, and without whose encouragement I would not have survived?"

The answer to both those unspoken questions was a resounding "Yes". The spirit of comradeship created by our common experience was as strong as ever, and we had a fantastic ten days. Through a continuous programme of events, concerts and visits, with a grand parade to the Shrine of Remembrance on the Sunday, we were surrounded by men whose names came back to me vividly after a gap of forty years, by the wives they had met and married in the interval, and by others who had gathered there from Canada, Holland, New Zealand, the States and the UK. Harold Payne, our President, was there, Les and Pam Stubbs from Birmingham, and Jim Bradley — who had written an account of his attempted escape from the Railway, called *Towards the Setting Sun* — with his wife, Linda. There were Australian St Dunstaners who knew of us through the *Review* and were glad to put a voice to a name: Bob Rolls, whose wife Dawn had met us — as dawn was breaking! — on arrival, and Allan Gee, a survivor from HMAS *Perth* which had been sunk in the Sunda Strait on 28 February, 1942, and his wife, Kath. We also met Hugh Clarke who had just written a book entitled *Last Stop Nagasaki* which was launched in grand style in front of the Press and TV cameras, an affair at which I was suddenly called upon to say a few words. And my saviour, protector and friend, Weary Dunlop, was there and took us out to dinner, then to meet his wife, Helen, and his son, Alexander.

I didn't, however, get away without having to sing for my supper. In the — then — brand-new Melbourne Concert Hall, during a mixed and deeply nostalgic programme of songs and sketches — the "Changi Prison Concert Party", performing together for the first time for forty years — we were on the bill, and I sang the song, *Sincerity*, which had originally been taught me by an Australian POW. Then Alice and I sang a couple of duets together. Altogether, an evening which would have meant little to anyone who hadn't been a prisoner of the Japanese, but to those who had, enough to bring tears as well as laughter.

Two years later there was a replay, this time at Broadbeach, near Brisbane, up on the coast of Queensland. Again Alice and I had hesitation about going, not because of any doubts about the welcome we should be given, but on grounds of expense. The return flight for the two of us, plus hotel and incidental expenses for a fortnight, would amount to a formidable sum, and one which we really couldn't afford. However, after much calculation and working out of sums on the backs of envelopes, we said, to hell with it, we'll go. The temptation was too strong to resist. (I must say here that although the basic reason for attending these reunions is obviously my involvement with Far Eastern Prisoners of War, and the boost to my spirits they always give, Alice never complains about having to come too. Not that complaining would do her much good! Luckily, though, she's an outgoing, sociable person who enjoys meeting new people, so perhaps it's not as tedious for her as it sounds, having to listen to us old buffers swapping endless yarns about eating rice and seaweed, and that diabolical Jap guard in Tandjong Priok!)

So, anyway, we decided to go, and hang the expense. Then, a squadron of good fairies came flying through the window, or rather the letter-box. The first from the then Aussie POW President, George Beard, told us that Qantas Airways had offered to fly us out and back for nothing; the second announced that two anonymous Australian businessmen were prepared to help meet our hotel expenses for the entire two weeks. Well, I was flabbergasted, and so was Alice. Such generosity was amazing; it certainly amazed me, whose notion of "generosity" had been limited to a free ticket to the local cinema with my grandfather. Together, these two extremely handsome gestures meant that we could go without any worries.

Once there, the story was the same all over again: boundless hospitality, a round of engagements, more old pals, more yarns, more new friends. At this time Weary was putting together for publication his wartime diaries, and he introduced us to his editor at Thomas Nelson, Lady Ebury. His diaries, an agonizingly vivid day-to-day account of life, disease and, all too often, death in Japanese hands, and of his superhuman efforts to save lives, especially on the notorious Thailand-Burma railway, were published in Australia that same year, and in England in 1987. With him and Lady Ebury we flew to Sydney to be interviewed at short notice by Ray Martin on TV, and then back to Brisbane the same evening for the Reunion Concert. Altogether, it was quite a day — and quite a fortnight.

Between these two Australian visits we were invited to an American ex-Prisoner of War Convention in Milwaukee, Wisconsin, where I was to represent Harold Payne, our National President. The atmosphere was very different, more formal than our FEPOW reunions, perhaps because in America all ex-POWs — 86,000 of them — belong to one organization, with a National Commander, three senior National Vice-Commanders, State and Chapter Commanders, and a Board of Directors. Wives are members and have voting rights. As I wrote in the *Review* afterwards, "The Convention is very serious; they get down to business at 8.30a.m. to 12 o'clock, back at 1pm until 4pm or later" — with no breaks for a cup of tea or coffee. There appeared to be nothing comparable to our St Dunstan's. Blind ex-servicemen and women are dependent on Government and State veterans administrations in common with other disabled ex-service people. I couldn't help thinking how fortunate we are to have the support of Sir Arthur Pearson's enlightened vision of the needs of the war-blinded. There were no blind veterans at Milwaukee, and only three men in wheelchairs.

In such able-bodied company I might have felt like a fish out of water, but in fact our hosts could not have been kinder or more attentive. I was swept off to be interviewed on radio and television, and at the Memorial Service was asked to sing. I chose "The Captive's Hymn", which had been introduced to me by our parson friend, Ray Rossiter, who had invited

210

me to sing it in Manchester Cathedral after one of our annual FEPOW parades. This hymn was written and composed by a woman prisoner of the Japanese, Margaret Dryburgh, who died in captivity, and I have sung it often since. The first verse goes:

> "Father, in captivity
> We would lift our prayer to Thee;
> Keep us ever in thy love,
> Grant that daily we may prove
> Those who place their trust in Thee
> More than conquerors may be."

In addition, Alice and I were asked to sing on a couple of occasions, once after a rather splendid lunch at a German restaurant, to which we were invited by the Australian National President, George Beard. We were to meet him and his wife again the following year in Brisbane. A good lunch is not the best training for a song, however!

Perhaps the thing that most clearly underlined the differences between an American affair of this kind and, say, a British or Australian one, was the fact that these ex-prisoners of war appeared to be wearing, so Alice told me, a kind of uniform, consisting of a forage cap, and waistcoats in maroon and gold depicting their state or chapter, the name of which was embroidered on the back and the officers wore a similar rig in white and gold. It all seemed a world away from the Japanese prison camp on Luzon or those, like Omuta, on Kyushu, where many Americans were incarcerated, as it was from Changi or Boe Glodok or the infernal jungle camps along the bitter road to Hellfire Pass. Yet, for the Americans as for the rest of us, the memories were indelible.

xiii

In April, 1987, Alice and I were off again on our travels, our immediate destination Thailand. We had been there, on holiday once before, in 1982, with the Blackpool FEPOW Club members but this time there were two reasons for the expedition, one frivolous, and one serious: it was to be a holiday with a purpose, for during our stay in Thailand we were to visit the Hellfire Pass Memorial, which had just been completed, and was to be dedicated on Sunday 26 April. The address was to be given by Weary, who had written to us earlier in the year encouraging us to come.

The background to the project, as every FEPOW — and the whole world — knows, was the construction between October, 1942 and October, 1943 of the Burma-Thailand railway, the notorious "Railway of Death". In mid-1942 the Japanese High Command decided that a link was needed between the railhead at Ban Pong in Siam, as it then was, and that at Thanbyuzayat, near Moulmein, in Burma, in order to supply their armies driving westwards to India. Because of the assertion of US naval superiority after the Battle of Midway in June, and Allied attacks on Japanese shipping in the Bay of Bengal, it was to be constructed at top speed.

212

The distance was 170 miles; the country was jungle-covered mountains rising to 3000 feet and cut by ravines; the method was much the same as that by which the Egyptians built the pyramids: a vast horde of slave labour, a total disregard for human life, and only the most basic hand-tools. The Japanese, who had not signed the Geneva Convention governing the treatment of prisoners-of war, and had no camps in which to put the thousands of Allied servicemen they had captured, immediately started drafting them up country to work on the railway. Of the 60,000 Australian, British, Dutch and Americans involved, 16,000 died through malnutrition, disease and brutal treatment. In addition, as many as 200,000 Asians — Tamils, Malays and Burmese — were employed, and of that number half, or more, also died. "On the railway itself," Geoffrey Pharoah Adams, who was there, writes, "it was said that for every sleeper laid, a man died. Japanese casualties were almost nil."

Because the orders of the High Command were that the line was to be constructed and carrying traffic within eighteen months, and this was later reduced to twelve — hence the murderous "*speedo*" — the men were forced to work shifts of anything up to eighteen hours at a stretch; at night the work continued by the light of flares and fires. Of all the stretches of that nightmare line, one has come to symbolize all the rest, the series of deep cuttings through the living rock which became known as "Hellfire Pass". The commemoration booklet issued to us by the Australian-Thai Chamber of Commerce, which co-ordinated the

213

project, describes work on the Konyu cutting in the following words:

> The excavation of soil and solid rock for the cuttings to a depth of 20 metres was completed with the use of minimal equipment. The prisoners were provided with 8-lb hammers, steel tap drills, dynamite, picks, shovels, wide hoes and small cane baskets . . . The excavation and the manhandling of the rock and soil of Hellfire Pass was carried out under intense pressure from the Japanese engineers and Korean guards at the height of the wettest monsoon season for many years.

No effort of the imagination by those who were not there can recreate the suffering of those men, but the Hellfire Pass Memorial, a stretch of the original line which includes the Konyu Or "Hammer and Tap" cutting, "will serve as a memorial to the thousands of lives so tragically sacrificed in the construction of the Burma-Thailand railway and to the Thai people who risked their lives to supply medicines and food to the prisoners during those dangerous times."

At the time, of course, none of us in Java knew of this, and I wasn't involved. I wouldn't have been much use to anyone if I had been! Yet everyone, men and women, European, American, Australian, New Zealand or Asian, who was in Japanese hands during those years, can understand and share the memory of that experience, however greatly it varied in its degree of physical and mental torture, of hunger, misery and deprivation. For this reason if for no other I was pleased to be going. But there were other reasons; the usual one, the prospect of meeting old friends and comrades; the opportunity of revisiting Thailand and of being present at the inauguration of a Medical Exchange Fellowship between Australia and the countries of South-East Asia which was to be named after Sir Edward Dunlop and Boon Pong, the river trader who supplied Weary with scarce, invaluable drugs. In his *War Diaries* Weary refers several times to "that magnificent man, Boon Pong" and his "wonderful services", and now, forty years later, that remarkable liason, which saved many lives, was to bear fruit in the form of a fellowship to promote and encourage medical knowledge and surgical skills between those countries. It too would be a form of memorial "to the futility of war". On 25 April, ANZAC day, a Service of Remembrance was held there in memory of those Australians and New Zealanders who had died, not only here, but wherever the campaigns of the two World Wars had been fought, from Flanders to Gallipoli, and from Crete to New Guinea.

To return to Singapore in 1982 had been, for me, a strange and rather exciting experience. Perhaps because it was almost the last place I had actually seen with my own eyes and my last few weeks there had been so horrendous — driving through air raids, dodging machine-gun attacks and burning oil tanks, diving into ditches and open drains — my memories of it were particularly vivid: memories good and bad. Three of my companions, Reg Dunne, Bert Ogden and Ned Peake, had been with me then and when we visited the Raffles Hotel they reminded me that it was they who had been ordered to smash all the bottles to prevent their contents going down Japanese throats. How much this contributed to the defeat of the Japanese is difficult to say, but it certainly lowered their spirits! One pleasure, which Alice did not share, was a good dish of Nasi Goreng, but then it doesn't have the same associations for her as it has for me.

From Singapore we went by train to Kuala Lumpur and on to Penang. This was pure holiday, sun, sea and sand, apart from a visit to the Commonwealth War Graves Cemetery at Taiping, on the mainland, the last resting place of a thousand POWs and still, so the others said, beautifully kept. Back at the hotel on the island we found ourselves surrounded by Japanese tourists, and Alice asked me,

"Does the sound of all their chatter upset you?"

"Not a bit," I said, "as long as they're not armed with bamboo truncheons and don't intend to start using them!"

"It's all right," Alice said, "they're not carrying anything more lethal than cameras."

"That's all right then," I said. In fact, to hear that strange, unintelligible, lisping tongue again after all these years and in these pleasantly luxurious conditions only underlined the fact of being free. So clear, yet so remote, was that other time, it was hard to believe that these were the same people — possibly some of them the very same people — who had teased and slapped and punched me, taken my stick from me, and asked me in that tone of cold inquiry, "Why you live?"

From Penang we were flown to Bangkok, and went from there by train to the Rama River Kwai Hotel which is only a short walk from the War Graves Cemetery at Kanchanaburi, where nearly 7000 of those who died on the railway are buried.

On the visit in 1984 we were taken by coach to the Memorial itself. The railway, built at such a cost, is now mainly disused, but the line of it can still be followed, some of the original sleepers are still to be found — each one a human life — and steps and walkways have been constructed to enable visitors to gauge for themselves what a monumental achievement, both in human and engineering terms, this railway was. There is already a museum and a memorial plaque, and, in the second phase of the project, a trail will lead to Hintok Bridge, known as "Pack of Cards Bridge" because, as the booklet describes, it "collapsed three times during construction, and was constructed in three weeks out of unseasoned timber fastened with wooden pegs, spikes, bamboo ties and rattan rope." Whether the collapses were due to deliberate sabotage by the builders is not stated, but I seem to remember hearing somewhere that this was the case.

Although the distances were not great, there were an awful lot of steps and the weather was hot and humid, but Alice managed to guide me and herself the full distance, and, as there were several chaps in the party who had actually worked on the railway and could describe the ground, I was able to get a vivid picture in my mind of just what they had gone through. Now State Highway 323 runs close by, there is a River Kwai Village Hotel and it is becoming a tourist attraction. In the light of the film, it is amusing to note that no bridge over the River Kwai itself was built during the construction of the railway and the film was made, not in Thailand, but in Ceylon.

After all these exertions, it was pleasant to spend our last few days in the country at the seaside resort of Pattaya, on the south-east coast, with nothing more energetic being demanded of us than wallowing in the sea, and going for a ride on an elephant. And if, at the end of it all, we found our emotions in some turmoil, that was hardly surprising, enjoyment of the present clashing with a deep sadness for all that we had heard and for all the lives that had been destroyed or ruined or cut short by that desperate and brutal enterprise.

Well, that's about it. Below me, as I sit here in my study — we live on the first floor — is our garden. I can only picture it from what I've been told, but I know that it is square, with grass in the middle and a paved path all round the edge. When I feel the need for fresh air and a bit of exercise, I can go downstairs, let myself out of the garden door, and follow the path: twenty paces, — though I never count them, or stairs either — turn left; twenty paces, turn left again; and so on, round and round, knowing that I shan't bump into anything or lose my bearings. It may not sound much, but it's important, one of the things on that not very extensive list which is my charter of independence.

218

All round me in the study are the machines which make up some of the most vital items on that list, and which I've described already. In order to write this I have slipped my stumps into the sockets of the extensions which, with their metal rods, enable me to type — though I had to ask Alice, who was busy in the kitchen across the hall, to put the paper into the machine for me. That's something I can't do, though I can move from room to room quite safely, even if I tend to keep my arms — my "bumpers" — extended in front of me, just in case. And, thanks, to the Air Commodore, I can go to the loo without having to shout for help!

In all blind people, I think, their other senses if they work at it, tend to develop to compensate for the one they have lost, especially hearing and touch. My hearing and sense of smell, as Alice has described, are acute and my sense of distance and direction when we are walking or driving surprises people. It's as if the map of where we are going unrolls in my mind and it is connected to some kind of mental tachygraph or milometer. In any case, my memory is excellent. It has to be. I do miss the sense of touch, though. I know of blind people who like to run their fingers over things to judge their shape and texture, and over the faces of their loved ones, and through that contact get a mental picture of them. I would love to be able to do that.

Too bad! Long, long ago I learnt that to bemoan the loss of what you can never have is a certain guarantee of disappointment, frustration and unhappiness, and what you have to do is make the most of whatever you

219

do have. Thanks to St Dunstan's, to our family, innumerable friends and relatives and neighbours, thanks, above all, to Alice, I have been able to do that, with the result that I have had a far fuller, richer life than I would have believed possible in the years immediately after my disablement. In those early days, both in POW camp and after I came home, I was often near despair, yet never quite slipped over the edge into the Slough of Despond. Except at the beginning, in the hospital in Bandoeng, when the pain was so frightful, I have never felt like giving up. Never since then have I felt like asking someone to "put me out". Having nothing to do, no sense of purpose, was the worst part. Idleness for me, and I suspect for many other people, is what really gets you down.

A strong constitution and a basically cheerful outlook have been my greatest assets, I think, but without Alice to encourage me, to support me with her enthusiasm and humour and no-nonsense care and, yes, her love and devotion, my life would have been very different. I wouldn't have learnt to sing, for one thing, and singing, even more than sport, has helped to fill my life with activity, with friends from many countries and all walks of life, and give it that saving sense of purpose, of contributing something, however modest, to the needs and joys of others.

Yes, strange as it may sound, coming from someone for whom most people automatically feel sorry, I can say honestly that I have been lucky.

And two last thoughts, the first from Alice:

One evening we were in a hotel in Blackburn, one of five hotels we had visited the same evening with RNIB officials. Billy was standing with them thanking a large audience for money raised throughout the year, as he had done at the other four hotels. I was standing at the back of the room, and a young couple near me, who had no idea that Bill and I even knew each other, and I heard the girl say to her companion, "Do you realize that that man" — nodding towards Bill — "gave all that for us, so that we can be free to be together, enjoying ourselves?" Coming from young people who knew nothing of the war except what they'd been told, I thought that was splendid.

The second from Bill's collaborator:

"The lass who retyped a number of pages of the manuscript said, 'I wish I'd had time to read it all. Even the bits I did read made me feel, What have I got to grumble about? They really cheered me up.'"

Postscript

Return to Java

In April/May, 1988, soon after finishing the book, I went back to Java. The trip was organized by the Java FEPOW Club (1942), and in the party — which included Alice, and Bob and Christine — were several old friends who had been with me in those dark days.

Our Air Canada flight took us to Singapore. Alice and I had visited it twice before, so there were no memories there which I had not already faced: on the previous occasions I had relived the six months before and during the Japanese invasion. Java was going to be another matter. At Singapore I had still been the lad from Blackburn, sound in wind and limb, while Java held my last reminders of a world I could touch and see. Why had I agreed to go back? Everything that had happened to me there was, you might think, best forgotten: everything, that is, except the love and care of friends and comrades who had helped me to survive; everything except the memory of those who had died there, while I had lived.

From Singapore we flew by Garuda Airlines to Jakarta, a short trip of only an hour and a half. There, as throughout our tour, we were met and taken care of:

and we were introduced to our guide, Jamal, who stayed with us throughout, spoke excellent English, had a wide knowledge of the world, and seemed able to persuade even the most suspicious security guards to allow us into the places we wanted to visit.

On our first full day of sightseeing — if that's the right word — we were taken by coach to Glodok, where there had been a POW camp; but the site was now occupied by a department store. From there we went to Kemayoran airfield. Bob Chapman, who had been in the party of POWs the Japs set to filling the bomb craters, said it was almost unchanged, even to the shrubbery where the Hurricanes flown ashore — too late — had been dispersed and destroyed.[1] Our next call was at Tanjong Priok, the harbour where we had disembarked after the horrendous voyage from Singapore. The guards did not want to let us in, but Jamal did his stuff so well that they tried to make us accompany them on a conducted tour, when all we wanted to do was have a look.

"That's where we landed, Bill," Frank Jackson said, "over there. We're walking over the very same ground we did then." And it seemed as if the years between had never been, and I could hear the frantic shouting, the bombs going off all round us, could sense the chaos and futility of it all.

---

[1] By coincidence, my co-author, Hugh Popham, had been in HMS *Indomitable* which had flown those aircraft off from her flight-deck; so he and I were probably a hundred miles or so apart at that time.

That was vivid enough, but it was part of that previous life which was now hardly more than a faint memory; a time when I had been able to enjoy the sight of the luxuriant countryside with its abundance of flowering trees and shrubs, instead of having to have it described to me. Much was as one remembered it, Hedley Bonnes said, as we retraced the road to Garut along which Frank Jackson and I had set out to rescue the two hundred stranded RAF men just before the capitulation; but there were changes too, the most noticeable being that the sarong, which had been almost universal, had virtually disappeared. Everyone now was in western dress. I decided I would rather keep my picturesque memories.

One day we visited the school which Weary and the others had turned into No. 1 Allied General hospital, and where I had been taken after the explosion. It seemed incredible to be back there, blind and handless, and yet having had, thanks to Weary, more than forty years of a fairly full life. No wonder he regards me as one of his success stories!

But of all the places we visited on our tour none made such an impression on me, or amazed the others so much, as the two ex-POW camps, St Vincentius and Tjimahi, where I had spent so many months. St Vincentius, we found, was still there and a convent school once again, and there was great excitement when we at last discovered it. The priest in charge let us wander about, and I found I was able to retrace the route along which I had tapped my way with my Heath Robinson gadget. I found the isolation room where we were deposited when we had dysentery, the place near the door where I had slept, and the flight of stairs where I had taken that purler. I was even able to lead the others to the hut where Colonel Maisey had given me the job of crushing herbs for the Dutch doctor. Yet more than forty years had passed, and I had never *seen* any of these places.

It was the same at Tjimahi. I was astonished to find that I remembered the slopes and turnings which led into the building and along the corridors to my old bed-space. And as I followed those old, horribly familiar trails — but this time with Alice's arm tucked firmly into mine — past and present became utterly confused. I *knew* that now I was safe in the company of my wife and friends, yet could I be quite certain that, at any moment, a Jap guard might not stop me and start bawling at me? As a reminder, behind the hospital was the army barracks where, if the war had not ended as abruptly as it did, I and all other POWs were to have been massacred.

Strangely enough, when I rejoined the rest of the party at the hospital gates, they told me that they had been talking to an old chap who, when he heard that we were ex-POWs, hurriedly made some excuse and fled. Apparently he was Japanese, and had been one of the officers in charge of us. He hadn't been keen to renew our acquaintance, it seemed! We weren't able to find the other camps we'd been in, but these four had been quite enough to stir up all the old memories which I have tried to describe in the book, and to bring back to mind the friends and comrades who had shared them, especially those whose bones rested in Menteng Pulo Cemetery.

We visited it for the first time on the second day of our tour, and I laid a wreath of poppies at the foot of the memorial cross, with a card which read: "The Java FEPOW Club, 1942. We remember." Then, on the night before we left Jakarta, four of us went back to pay our final respects. Among the crosses we found one to Captain John Rae Smith. He and I had had a bad bout of dysentery at the same time. He had died; here was I, standing by his grave. I felt deeply humble at the memory of all that loss and suffering, and deeply grateful for having been given the chance to return, for, truly, we do remember.

Appendix

In addition to those already mentioned in the book, many people from all walks of life have been a great encouragement to me; many are unaware of their help, some with their own problems, but still considering others. Firstly I must pay tribute to my friends of the Handless Reunion, in particular our two ladies, Gwen Obern and Winnie Edwards, also to Air-Vice Marshal Edward Colahan and Mrs Colahan, who, along with Mrs Dacre, do everything possible to make sure that we enjoy ourselves at our Reunion. St Dunstan's ex POW Reunion is another source of strength. Captain Harry Whitehead and George Pollard first introduced me to the Royal British Legion and, as a result, I have visited many branches, counties, etc., and made many friends. Harry Whitehead's is one of the voices I always recognize every Remembrance Sunday when assembling on Horse Guards' Parade. Blackpool Town Council and staff are always ready to be helpful. They and members of the Comrades Club have made me feel a "Sandgrown Un".

St Dunstan's Chairman, Admiral of the Fleet Sir Henry Leach, is a great influence. When he and Lady Leach came to Blackpool in October, 1987, our friends

Keith and Margaret Gledhill took care of them. Sir Henry and Lady Leach officially opened a new Wardroom at the Blackpool Sea Cadet H.Q. Mr J.L. Herdman is the Blackpool President; Sir Henry Leach is the National President of the Sea Cadets Association. Sir Henry and Lady Leach were the principal guests at the Festival of Remembrance given by the Ashton-on-Mersey Youth Showband, Musical Director Mr Ernie Waite. When Sir Edward Dunlop came later, I didn't feel so helpless as I knew that Keith was using his eyes and hands for me. On such occasions he takes the responsibility.

To witness people who care always gives me a spiritual uplift: to name but a few — Ernest Beeston, Arnside; Ian Magaw, former Conservative Candidate for Blackburn, now of Henley-on-Thames; Cousins Frank, Betty and Philip Smith of Bispham; Stephanie Cole, actress (doctor in T.V. Drama *Tenko*); John Burke, Hereford; the late Joe Castle, Morley, Leeds; William Griffiths Court committee and warden, Mrs D. Jepson; officials and members of all ex-service organizations and disabled groups; the Blackpool and Fylde Society for the Blind Council and staff; Blackpool and Blackburn Talking Newspaper for the Blind readers and production teams, as well as sportsmen and women and many celebrities that I have met.

Of course nearest to my heart are my St Dunstan's colleagues and staff, past and present, and FEPOW And Royal British Legion friends and officials.

230

I am grateful to friends abroad who have shown me great kindness and affection. The American ex-POW Federation International Co-ordinator, Harold Page and his wife, Virginia, from Seattle; Joe Galloway, past National Commander and his wife, Charlotte, from Florida, and many other friends.

My thanks to many friends in the Australian ex-POW Federations, to Jack and Betty Holmes, Ivor and Cath Jones and all members of the RAAF Malaya Association — Jim and Betty Boyle, Bluey and Lesley Butterworth and Jack Flanagan and so many more friends who have given me such encouragement and pleasure.

My sincere thanks to anyone who has helped me by word or deed. It is impossible to mention everyone. You know in your heart your contribution. As I write this an incident comes to mind. After the TV programme *This Is Your Life* was transmitted, a very good friend rang to congratulate me. I apologized to him for his not being included with the guests. He simply said, "We know what we did in those days. It doesn't have to be said on T.V., Billy." He was right in his heart and that's what matters, to be right with oneself.

Also available in ISIS Large Print:

The Long Way Home

John McCallum

"Not many POWs had the good fortune to have a big brother to look after them in such circumstances, and to think he was there because of me made me feel terribly guilty at times."

At the age of 19, Glasgow-born John McCallum signed up as a Supplementary Reservist. By the middle of September 1939, he was in France, working frantically to set up communication lines after the outbreak of war. Wounded and captured, he was sent to the notorious Stalag VIIIB prison camp, together with his brother, Jimmy, and friend Joe Harkin.

The three men set about planning their escape. With the help of a local girl, they put their plan into action. In an astonishing coincidence, they passed through the town of Sagan, around which the 76 airmen of the "Great Escape" were being pursued and caught. However, unlike most of these other escapees, John, Jimmy and Joe eventually made it to freedom.

ISBN 0-7531-9370-1 (hb)
ISBN 0-7531-9371-X (pb)

In Action with the SAS

Roy Close

". . . the story of one individual who, when circumstances required, put down his clerk's pen, took up a weapon and, like many others, spent six and a half years in uniform."

Already a member of the Territorial Army, Roy was mobilised in 1939 and joined the British Expeditionary Force in France. After three days and two nights on the Dunkirk beaches he was evacuated back to England.

He was then sent to North Africa and a chance meeting resulted in his transferring to the newly formed Parachute Regiment and, from there, the elite Special Air Service.

In 1944 he was infiltrated into German-occupied France where he operated with the Maquis resistance organisation. During the closing stages of the War the scene shifts to Holland and the advance through Germany. The author describes life in newly liberated Paris and Berlin in the early post-war years.

ISBN 0-7531-9364-7 (hb)
ISBN 0-7531-9365-5 (pb)